365
AFTER-SCHOOL ACTIVITIES

you can do with your child

Safety Reminder for Parents and Children

The activities in this book are intended for children between ages 5 and 10, and some of them may be unsafe for younger children. Regardless of the child's age, parents should provide appropriate supervision for the activities, taking into account the child's age and experience. In particular, parents and children should be award of the following safety concerns:

- Some of the activities make use of the stove or oven. Parents should provide appropriate supervision.

- Some of the activities make use of scissors, needles, push pins, and other sharp objects. Make sure the child knows how to use them safely.

- Some of the activities make use of empty cans and wire hangers. Make sure there are no sharp or protruding edges.

- Some of the activities make use of substances that can be harmful if swallowed, including bluing and detergent.

365
AFTER-SCHOOL
ACTIVITIES

you can do with your child

by Cynthia MacGregor

Adams Media Corporation
Holbrook, Massachusetts

Published by
Adams Media Corporation
260 Center Street, Holbrook, MA 02343

ISBN: 1-58062-212-7

Printed in Canada.

J I H G F E D C B

Library of Congress Cataloging-in-Publication Data
MacGregor, Cynthia.
365 after-school activities / Cynthia MacGregor.
p.   cm.
ISBN 1-58062-212-7
1. Creative activities and seat work. 2. Activity programs in education.
I. Title: Three hundred sixty-five after-school activities.
LB1027.25.M23   1999
372.5—dc21   99-27507
CIP

Purchase and use of this book constitutes acceptance of the following
conditions: that all activities herein contained are to be conducted with
appropriate adult supervision; that due care will be exercised by parents
and/or guardians in selection of activities, especially with regard to the age
appropriateness of the activity; and that the publisher shall be in no way
liable for any adverse actions or mishaps arising directly or indirectly from
inadequately supervised activities, or from adverse actions or mishaps
arising from instructions included in any part of this book.

Cover photograph by FPG International/Daniel Pangbourne.

This book is available at quantity discounts for bulk purchases.
For information, call 1-800-872-5627.

Visit our home page at http://www.adamsmedia.com

Dedication

For Laurel and family

Acknowledgments

Thanks especially to Vic Bobb, as always. Thanks also to Ken Wilson. And grateful thanks to the others who gave me ideas for this book but asked that they not be mentioned by name.

Table of Contents

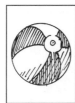

17: Beep!

18: Beyond Pig Latin

19: Big Talkers

20: Big-Circle Beanbag

21: Biking to DisneyWorld®

22: Blank Jigsaw Puzzles

23: Blottos

24: Blow Soap Bubbles

25: Bottle-Cap Basketball

26: Boxed In

27: Braided Heart

Button Box Fan image

28: Button Box Fan

29: Buzz

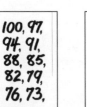

30: By Threes . . . Backward

31: A Calendar Just for Fun

32: A Calendar of Your Child's Own

33: Candy 'n' Cake

34: A Carton of Fun—1

35: A Carton of Fun—2

36: A Carton of Fun—3

37: Catch My Act!

38: Checker Chase

39: Checker Roll

40: Chests to Treasure

41: Chinese-Style Screen

42: Clay Miniatures

43: Clock Solitaire

44: Clown Wall Hanging

**45: Coded Messages
"By the Book"**

46: Collage Box

47: Collect Odd Facts

**48: Comical Books 1—
Words First**

**49: Comical Books 2—
Pictures First**

50: Complete-a-Story

51: Control Panel

52: Crab Soccer

**53: Crayon-Stub
Stained Glass**

54: Create a Board Game

55: Create a Cityscape

56: Create a Garland

57: Create a Rebus

58: Critters

**59: Custom-Designed
Jewelry**

**60: Design a Flag for
Your Hometown**

**61: Design and Name
a Car**

62: Designer Lunch Bags

**63: Do Play with
Your Food!**

64: Domino Knockdown

65: Domino Match-Ups

66: Domino Solitaire

67: Don't Laugh

68: Dr. Dolittle

69: Draw a Treasure Map

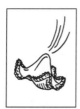

70: Drop the Hankie

71: Dry-Land Fishing

72: Duck Duck Goose

73: Dynomatic Implosionary Elfranginating Ray Blaster

74: Early Speller Safari

75: Earth-Friendly Living

76: Edible Necklace

77: Egg-Carton Caterpillar

78: Eggshell Mosaics

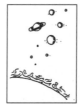

79: The Eighth Dwarf? The Tenth Planet?

80: Family Flower . . . and Bird, and Tree

81: Family Portrait Gallery

82: Family Suggestion/ Treat Box

83: Family Timeline 1— Simple Version

84: Family Timeline 2— Extended Version

85: Family Timeline 3— Multiple Version

86: Find-a-Fact Safari

87: Fine Design

88: Fingerprint Drawings

89: Fishbowls

90: Five Hundred

91: Fizz

92: Fizz-Buzz

93: Flipping Cards

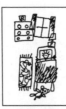
94: Floor Plans

95: Flying Shuffleboard

96: Flying Tropical Fish

97: Football-Card Football

98: Forbidden Letters

99: Form a Rock Band . . . with Action Figures

100: Fortune-Egg-ly

101: Four-Sense Descriptions

102: Fresh, Hot Tarantulas

103: Frisbee Golf

104: Funny Names

105: Geography

106: Ghost

107: Ghosts in the Mansion

108: Glamour Makeover

109: Go Surfing (on the Net)

110: Grass Whistle

111: The Great Detective

112: Grounded Jump-Rope Game 1

 113: Grounded Jump-Rope Game 2

 114: "Grow" an Indoor Garden

 115: "Grow" New Crayons

 116: Guess the Number

 117: Gumdrop Drop

 118: Handprint Tulips

 120: Hanging Jack-o'-Lantern

119: Hang a Motto or Banner

 121: Happy Judy Day!

 122: Heart-Themed Wrapping Paper

 123: Hey—I'm Oprah!

 124: Hippopotamus

 125: Holiday Braid

 126: Homemade Double Jigsaw Puzzle

 127: Homemade Greeting Cards

 128: Homemade Jigsaw Puzzles

129: Horse

130: House Number Math

131: Household Scavenger Hunt

132: How Knot to Be Bored

133: I "Can" Score— Indoors

134: I "Can" Score— Outdoors

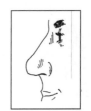

135: "I Have a Large Nose"

136: "I Make a Motion"

137: "I Want to Sell You a Kangaroo"

138: I.D. Game

139: If I Ruled the Island . . .

140: If Queen Isabella Met President Kennedy

141: Illustrate a Story

142: "I'm Going Shopping"

143: The Improv Game

144: The Incredible Adventures of Jon Green

145: Initials

146: Initials . . . Title . . . Story

147: Invent a Food

148: Invent a Game

149: Invent a Holiday— Version 1

150: Invent a Holiday— Version 2

151: Invent a New Dance

152: Invisible Ink Messages

153: Is It Comic? No, It's "Serial"

154: It Means What It Sounds Like

155: It's a Collyfluribus!

156: I've "Bean" to Boston

157: Jessica Originals

158: Jeweled Egg Ornaments

159: Jigsaw Books

160: Jigsaw Valentines

161: Join the Circus— at Home

162: Keep a Straight Face

163: Keeping It Uniform

164: Kick the Can

165: Kids Can Cook Too

166: Kings in the Corner

167: Knowledge Tag

168: Leaf People

169: A Letter to a Friend

170: Long Ago—When You Were a Kid

171: Magazine Letter Scavenger Hunt

172: Magazine Scavenger Hunt

173: Magic Garden of Jupiter

174: Make a Distinctive Vase

175: Make a Door Nameplate

176: Make a Pinwheel!

177: Make a Themed Collage

178: Make a Totem Pole

179: Make a Wishing Tree

180: Make Bookplates

181: Make Masks . . . Just for Fun—1

182: Make Masks . . . Just for Fun—2

183: Make Old-Fashioned Paper Dolls

184: Make the Connection

185: Making Book— Literally

186: Many Happy Returns . . . and Exchanges

187: Map Games— Stump Your Parents

188: Marble Roll

189: Match or Pay

190: Match or Pay— Odds and Evens

191: Measuring in Tony Feet

192: Miniature "Christmas Trees"

193: Mirror Drawing

194: Mirror Image

195: Mirror Tic-Tac-Toe

196: Mirror Walk

197: Mirror-Echo Name

198: Mix 'n' Match Proverbs

199: Mixies

200: Monkey in the Middle

201: Monogram Wall Decoration

202: Mosaic Nameplate

203: Mother, May I?

204: Mr. Hiss

205: My Friend Is a Real Dummy

206: "My Room!"

207: Name Challenges

208: Name Games— Anagrams and Word Yields

**209: Name Games—
Name Attributes**

**210: Natural "Canvas"
Painting**

**211: Nature Bingo—
Type I**

**212: Nature Bingo—
Type II**

**213: Neighborhood
Scavenger Hunt**

214: The New 15¢ Coin

**215: New Style Building
Blocks**

216: Nickel Golf

217: Nonsense Rhymes

218: Nonstop Talkers

219: Nuts for Boating!

**220: Occupied—and
Beyond**

**221: Odds 'n' Evens
Chase**

222: Official Forms

**223: Once upon a Time,
When I Was Invisible**

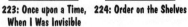

224: Order on the Shelves

**225: Organize
Your Books**

226: Paging Geraldo!

**227: Paging Geraldo . . .
Junior Grade**

228: Paper Beads

229: Paper Snowflakes

230: Party Prep

231: Patterned Snacks

232: Peeping at Peepers

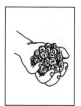

233: Penny Height

234: Penny Lag

235: Personalized Stationery

**236: Phone Number
Words**

237: Pick-a-Plot

238: Pictures on a Frame!

239: Pillow Tag

**240: Ping-Pong Pounce—
Competitive Version**

241: Ping-Pong Pounce—Solo Version

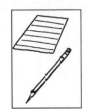

242: Plan to Start a Club

243: Plants of Ancient Times

244: Playing Office

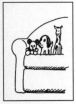

245: Playing to a Receptive Audience

"4 Out of 5 people said.."

246: Pollsters, Inc.

247: Popcorn Garlands

248: Potato Puppets

249: Presenting Our Newest DJ

250: Preserving Grandma's Stories

251: Printed Shelf Paper

252: Probabilities— with Cards

253: Probabilities— with Dice

254: Progressive Stories

255: P-T Fun

256: Publish a Neighborhood Newsletter

257: Puppet Theater—1

258: Puppet Theater—2

259: Questions

260: Quick-Think Categories

261: Ramp Bowling

262: "Ransom" Stories

263: The Real Story of . . .

264: Red Light, Green Light

265: Red Rover— Version 1

266: Red Rover— Version 2

267: A Report Card for Your Teacher

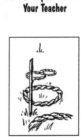

268: Reverse Silhouette

269: Rhythm Sticks

270: Riddle Squares

271: Ring Toss— Horseshoe Rules

272: Ring Toss— Quoits Rules

273: Robinson Radio Theatre

274: Rock, Scissors, Paper

275: Rockin' Santa

276: Roving Reporter

277: Rubber Band Knockdown

278: Ruler Challenge

279: Run, Sheep, Run

280: Sand Jars

281: Sardines

282: Sawtooth Trees

283: Score-a-Goal

284: Score-a-Name

285: Scrambled Words

286: Scrambled Words Plus

287: Scratch Paintings

288: Sears, Roebuck, and Annie

xxiv

289: Seed Mosaics

290: Send a Coded Message—1

291: Send a Coded Message—2

292: Sentence Ingredients

293: Shared Birthdays

294: Sheet Ball

295: Shooting Stars

296: The Silver Rule

297: Snail

298: Snow Jar

299: Solitaire Golf

300: Solo Scrabble™— Version 1

301: Solo Scrabble™— Version 2

302: Splash!

303: Stare Down

304: Start a Leaf Collection

305: Statues

306: Story-Time Turnabout

307: String Balloons

308: String Paintings

309: String Race

310: Stuck on You!

311: Survey Your Street

312: Syrup Painting

313: Talk Backward!

314: Target Rolling

315: Tell Me a Riddle . . . of Your Own Invention

316: Ten to Get the Word

317: Themed Chain

318: Themed Wastebasket

319: This Is My Universe

320: Thread-Spool Puppets

321: Throwing Money Around

322: Tie-Dyed Paper Towels

323: Timed Stroll

324: Today's Events— in Pictures

325: Tongue Twisters

326: Top Ten Lists

327: Top Ten Rules of . . .

328: Town Planner

329: Town-in-a-Hubcap

330: T-P Bowling

331: T-P Dachshunds

332: Trade-a-Book

333: Treat Hunt

334: Triangular Tug-of-War

335: A Trip from the Moon

336: A Trip to the Moon

337: Two-Card Drop

338: Unlocking the Secret

339: Unlucky Fives

340: Uno, Dos, Tres . . .

341: Untrue—in Any Words

342: Vegetables Prints

343: Very Icy

344: Very Short Stories

345: Walnut Mice

346: Waxed Garfield?

347: Weekly Wrap-Up

348: What Do You Say to That?

349: What's in a Name?

350: Who Was That Masked Man?

351: Whoozit Boxes

352: With a Critical Eye

353: A Wonderful Invention

354: Word Baffle

355: Word Chains

356: Word Lightning

357: Word Pictures

358: Word Search

359: Word Search— Variations

360: Write a Patriotic Song

361: Write Commercials

362: Yarn Vase

363: The (Your Name) Dictionary

364: Your Roving Reporter . . . on Mars

365: Zoo's Who?

Introduction

What's the first thing your child does when he or she comes home from school (well, after cookies and the bathroom)?

If your answer is "homework," you've got a very conscientious child. However, most kids need a cooling-off period after being set free from school for the day, before they're willing to dive into homework. If your answer is "watch TV," I'd like to make some alternative—and, I think, better—suggestions. And if your answer is "whine that he's bored," I definitely have some suggestions.

What's more, although the title of this book is *365 After-School Activities*, the "book police" aren't watching to make sure your child engages in these activities only after three on a school day. Weekends, school holidays, and days when he's home sick from school but not flat on his back in bed . . . all these are open season on the activities in this book.

A few words about what you'll find here:

First of all, there's a mix of activities for one child and for more than one, with many activities earmarked for one or more. If your child is an "only" who didn't bring a friend home from school, or a child whose siblings are busy with Scouts, band, gymnastics, or homework, he needn't whine that there's no one to play with. Maybe there isn't, but he can still find plenty to do within these pages.

You'll notice that I just said "he." Though I've arbitrarily used "he" and "she" within these pages, that isn't an indication that the activities in which I've used "he" are better suited for boys or the activities in which I've said "she" are better suited for girls. It's just an attempt to avoid the "he or she" construction. Don't read gender orientation into the pronouns.

And speaking of avoiding awkwardness, some descriptions of activities in this book are written as if I were addressing the person who's going to undertake them. Addressing parents by saying "Have your child do this" and "Tell your child to do that" can sometimes get awfully convoluted. Nonetheless, this is really a book to be read by parents rather than kids.

Some of the activities may not suit your child's age, temperament, or some other set of circumstances. Still others have notes of caution in them, such as when an activity calls for parental help to avoid hazard. And you'll want to pick the right activities for your child and for the circumstances. (For instance, select the activity about making party hats when it's getting close to your child's birthday.)

So take a browsing trip through the book. See the variety of activities that are offered. Get familiar with them. There are quiet and active activities, indoor and outdoor, artsy and athletic and otherwise, solo and with friends, with or without parental involvement—in short, something for every child, every mood, every situation, every day.

After you've read the book and have an idea of what's in here, turn your child loose to enjoy a different activity every day.

And I do mean enjoy. Have fun—it's an important part of life!

Accountant's Race

Players in this race get to do what accountants struggle to do all day long . . . balance books—all the way to the finish line.

Establish a start line and a finish line, and give each player, or each of the lead players in a relay race, a book to balance on his head. Players race from the start line to the finish line, but they must keep the books on their heads as they go. If a book falls, that player is out of the race. Hands must be kept below shoulder level at all times; holding the book in place is not permitted.

With two or three players, all race at the same time. With four or more players, you may want to run a relay race.

T W O
or more

MATERIALS

Two or three books

ONE

MATERIALS

A deck of cards
(bridge/poker)

Ace, Deuce, Three

Ever wished you could predict the future? In this game, you hope you can't! The rules of the game are very easy; winning is very difficult.

Shuffle an ordinary deck of cards and say, "Ace." Then turn the first card over. If it's anything but an Ace, say, "Deuce," and turn over the next card. Again, if it's anything but a deuce, say, "Three," and turn over a card . . . which, as you've gathered by now, you hope is not a three. Your "predictions" must always follow in order—you're not allowed to actually guess on your own. If you get all the way up to the King successfully, start all over at the ace, continuing to "predict" until you've gone through the entire deck (four rounds of Ace through King), or until you lose.

At any point, if the card you turn over is what you "predicted," you've lost, and the game is over. But if you can get all the way through the deck without the card you turn over being what you "predicted," you're a winner!

Ace of Towers

If you have a deck of cards whose 7 of diamonds has bent corners, or a deck that's missing the 10 of spades, don't throw it out. Give it to your junior construction engineer, along with a pair of scissors, and you have an easy tower-building project in the works.

Traditional towers of cards require that one card be balanced delicately on the next . . . just so. One wrong touch and the whole thing comes tumbling down. It's not a very educational pursuit: It teaches kids to cuss.

Here's a much less frustrating way to build with cards: Cut a half-inch slit right in the middle of each of the four sides of each card. Now build your tower or fort or other structure by interlocking the cards. Cutting the slits in the cards should keep your child busy for quite a while; actually constructing structures with the cards can keep her busy over many an afternoon after school (or on a rainy Saturday or school holiday).

O N E
or more

MATERIALS

✐ Deck of cards you were going to throw out, scissors (beginner's scissors are okay)

3

T W O

MATERIALS

✐ Part of a deck of cards

Add 'n' Capture

Play using the black cards from Ace through 6 and the red cards from 2 through King (Aces = 1, Jacks = 11, Queens = 12, Kings = 13).

Deal six cards to each player. Player 1 lays down two black cards. If he doesn't have two black cards, he lays down any red card faceup to start the discard pile and takes another card from the draw pile. If necessary, he continues till he can lay down two black cards.

If Player 2 has a red card that equals the sum of those two black cards (e.g., a red 9 to capture a black 4 and 5), he takes the two black cards and lays them down with his red card to start his bank pile. If Player 2 cannot capture the two cards, they go into the discard pile. Player 1 draws two more cards. If Player 2 was able to capture, he draws another card.

Now Player 2 plays two black cards and Player 1 tries to capture them. Continue back and forth. When the draw pile is exhausted, shuffle the discards and use them as a draw pile once more. Then the game ends. The player with the highest number (not value) of cards in his bank pile wins.

Add 'n' Subtract Solitaire

After shuffling, place the first four cards faceup, side by side, to start your display. Turn over three cards at a time from the deck, basic solitaire-style, playing the top card onto the display if possible, in any of these ways:

ONE

- Play a card on top of another of the same number.
- Play a card below two cards if it equals the difference between the value of the two (Aces = 1, Jacks = 11, Queens = 12, Kings = 13).
- Play a card above two cards if it equals the sum of the value of the two.

For example, if your display is 4 A 8 J, you may play:

- Another 4, A, 8, or J on top of the like cards
- A 5 above and between the 4 and A
- A 9 above and between the A and 8
- A 3 below and between the 4 and A
- A 7 below and between the A and 8
- A 3 below and between the 8 and J

If you can play the entire deck onto the display, you win.

MATERIALS

- A deck of cards (bridge, not pinochle)

Ala Kazam . . . Egg Witch

MATERIALS

Egg carton (cardboard is better than styrofoam), markers or construction paper, glue, scissors, yarn or dried weeds

You'll get a coven of witches—well, a terrible trio, anyhow—out of each egg carton. Start by removing the lid, then cutting the egg carton into three pieces, each consisting of a square of four egg cups. The instructions from here on are for one of these squares; repeat them on each of the segments you've cut, and you'll have your trio of witches.

It doesn't matter which way you hold your square of egg cups, but turn the two top cups into eyes either by gluing circles of colored paper into the bottoms of the cups or by drawing the eyes on with markers. (Marker may not hold on styrofoam; if your carton isn't made of cardboard, you may have only one option.) The bump in the middle is the witch's nose; you don't need to do anything to it, but you can draw two dots for nostrils on it if you want. Create the mouth by drawing a line from one lower cup to the other.

Glue either dried weeds or yarn (brown, tan, grey, or black are your best color choices) on the top of the head to create hair.

Alphabet Stories

Alphabet stories are a variation on Progressive Stories (page 254). But in this form of progressive story, every player contributes exactly one sentence to the story at a time . . . and the first letter of that sentence must be the letter that alphabetically follows the letter that began the preceding sentence.

It's not necessary to begin with A. The first player is free to begin anywhere. But if John's first sentence is, "Gary got lost on a trip through some caves in Colorado," then, because his sentence started with a G, Kenny's sentence, which follows, must start with an H. Kenny might say, "He was scared in the darkness, and his flashlight burned out quickly." Jennifer might add, "'I knew I should have brought more batteries,' he said." The next sentence might be, "Just then, he heard an eerie noise."

Players may choose in advance to omit sentences beginning with X and Z, or even U if they feel those will be problems.

The game is over when the story comes back to the letter of the alphabet it started with.

TWO
or more

MATERIALS

✎ None

7

Animal Encyclopedia Safari

O N E
or more

MATERIALS

Encyclopedia, paper, pen or pencil

To keep this from seeming like a homework assignment or (gasp!) an educational activity, you'll probably need to either turn it into a competition or offer an award. The basic idea is for the child to "capture" an animal by writing down five facts about it, as learned by reading about the animal in the encyclopedia (or another suitable reference book you may have around the house or at the library).

For a competition, turn two or more kids loose on the encyclopedia, give them a reasonable time limit, and then declare as the winner the child who has captured the most animals.

For a solo child, you may want to offer a reward for each animal captured or for capturing more than a certain number of animals.

The facts she writes down should not be common knowledge, such as "baby dogs are called puppies" or "cowboys in the Old West rode horses."

8

Backward Writing

Can you print the letters of your name backward? It isn't easy, but it's fun to try. Spell your name with the letters in their usual order, but draw the letters backward.

Try it both with all capitals and using uppercase and lowercase. Some capital letters are the same forward and backward, such as A or H, but their lowercase versions are not the same (a, h).

Try it while looking in a mirror and also without using a mirror. Which way is easier? Which way is more fun?

Can you write a whole sentence using backward letters? How about a note to a friend? Will your friend be able to read what you have written?

ONE
or more

MATERIALS

✏ Paper, pen or pencil

9

Balloon Football—Indoor Version

FOUR
or more

MATERIALS

✐ Balloons (one to play with, extras in case the first one accidentally gets popped), large table

Each team stands at one end of the table, with the "ball" in the middle. Players at all times use only their breath to try to knock the balloon off the opposing team's end of the table.

If any part of any player's body touches the balloon, it's a foul. In that event, place the balloon three-quarters of the way toward the end of the table closest to the team that committed the foul. One player from the opposing team then gets one puff at the balloon, after which normal play resumes.

"Touchdowns," worth 6 points, are scored by blowing the balloon off the opposite end of the table. The balloon is then placed three-quarters of the way toward the team that scored; one player tries to score an extra point by blowing it off the opposite end in one breath. No defensive maneuvers are permitted. After that, the balloon is re-placed in the table's center, and the other team kicks off.

If at any time the balloon is blown "out-of-bounds" (off the sides of the table), it is re-placed where it was blown off, and play resumes.

Balloon Football— Outdoor Version

Play Balloon Football outdoors on a section of driveway or pavement, chalk marking the boundaries of your playing field. To score a touchdown, blow the balloon into the end zone; there are no goalposts. There's no regulation size to the field; draw it whatever size you want or as space permits. The number of players may influence the size of field you draw, too.

No player may touch the balloon with any part of the body, even accidentally. If this does occur, it's a foul. Players who see the balloon approaching them should get out of the way even while blowing at it to deflect it from the goal and send it back in the other direction.

See the indoor version (on the preceding page) for rules regarding "out-of-bounds" and "touchdowns." To score the extra point, one player from the side that scored the touchdown stands in front of the balloon, which is placed 3 feet from the goal line, and tries to blow the balloon across the goal line with one breath.

As with indoor play, there are two fifteen-minutes halves, with teams switching sides at halftime.

G R O U P

MATERIALS

🖎 Balloons (one to play with, extras in case the first one gets popped by accident), chalk

MATERIALS

Balloon, long
piece of string

Balloon Volleyball

As in Balloon Football (the preceding two pages), no body parts may touch the ball.

Tie a string across a large open space (backyard, basement, park). If possible, the string should be at the height of most of the players' necks.

Each team tries to blow the balloon across the string, hoping it will fall to the ground on the other side. If it does, the team that blew it there scores a point, regardless of which side served the ball.

A player defending against an incoming ball may not use anything but his breath to keep the balloon aloft. If the balloon touches any part of a player's body (or clothing), it's a foul, and the other team scores a point.

When a team has scored, whether by grounding the ball on the opponents' side or by foul, one player from the other team puts the ball back in play. He holds it, standing at a point 6 feet behind the string. Then he blows it off his upraised hands. A similar procedure is used if the balloon drifts across under the string: The team that last had possession of it puts it back in play.

The first team to score 21 points wins.

Balloons That Never Pop

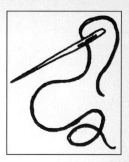

Here's a bunch of balloons that aren't vulnerable to a pin and that will never lose their inflation and sag, a bunch of color to decorate your child's room, and a cheery pick-me-up. Can your child sew? She can make her own balloons.

O N E

Fold a piece of fabric in half and cut two identical balloon shapes out of the double ply of fabric. Don't forget the balloon's neck. Hold the two halves together inside out and sew them together, on a sewing machine or by hand. Leave a little space unsewn at the base for stuffing the balloon.

Now turn the balloon right-side out and stuff it with cotton, foam, poly, or some other appropriate stuffing. Then finish sewing up the base.

When you have created several balloons, tack them together with a few stitches by hand in hidden places. Tie some yarn around the neck of each one, gathering the ends of the yarn together as you would with a bunch of real balloons.

Sew a ring near the top of the balloon and attach the balloons to a wall by hanging the ring from a nail or hook.

MATERIALS

- ✐ Bright-colored fabric (assorted colors, for making several balloons), yarn, needle and thread (for hand sewing), scissors, small metal or plastic ring, cotton batting or poly fiberfill or foam or other stuffing

- ✂ Optional: Sewing machine

13

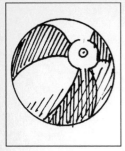

Beat the Ball

MATERIALS

✏ One ball,
preferably an
inflatable type,
though any kind
can be used

Form a large circle, with 6 or 8 feet separating each participant. Whoever happens to be holding the ball leads the game off by tossing the ball to the next player and, at the same time, breaking out of the circle. She takes off at a fast run around the outside of the circle.

Meanwhile, the other players pass the ball, throwing it from person to person to person, around the circle, while the runner continues sprinting around the outside of the circle. The object of the game is simply, as the name implies, for the runner to beat the ball around the circle and get back to her place in the circle before the ball gets back around.

The faster the other players toss the ball, the more likely it is that one of them will drop it. So while speed is important, it isn't everything.

After the first player has returned to her spot, the next player tries to beat the ball around the circle, whether or not the first person succeeded. There's no formal winner—each player simply tries to be a winner in her own turn, but the game's not competitive among players. The game may end when everyone's had a turn, or when everyone's had five turns, or just when the majority decide it's time to quit.

14

Beautify Your Neighborhood

O N E
or more

Here's a project your child can really feel good about. It may also teach him this valuable lesson: Don't litter; it makes your neighborhood ugly. So arm him with two empty garbage bags and a pair of work gloves, and send him around the block with these instructions:

Some people are slobs. But not you, right? You wouldn't throw candy wrappers or soda cans out in the street and make your neighborhood ugly, would you? Since some people, though, are totally thoughtless and dirty the neighborhood for those around them, you can help clean up.

Put all the nonrecyclable trash you find in one bag and all the recyclables you find in the other bag. If your neighborhood has a recycling center that pays for recyclables, you might even profit from this venture! But even if you don't profit financially, you'll profit by living in a cleaner neighborhood and in the satisfaction of knowing you did something meaningful to help this poor tired Earth, and your own neighborhood in particular.

MATERIALS

Work gloves; two empty, large garbage bags

15

GROUP

MATERIALS

✐ None

Beckon, Beckon, I Want a Beckon

Agree on boundaries; choose someone to be It. It covers his eyes and counts to 100; the others hide. Calling "Ready or not, here I come," It starts searching for hidden players. When It finds a hider— let's say it's Tori—the two race to Home Base. If It gets there first, he touches base and yells, "One-two-three on Tori." Tori is "imprisoned" at Home Base.

When It, seeking other hiders, is out of range, Tori may yell, "Beckon, beckon, I want a beckon." Any hidden player may wave, whistle, or call. Once Tori sees or hears the beckon, she runs and hides again. Any other imprisoned player who sees or hears it may also re-hide.

But if It sees or hears, It can find and catch that player. And if It spots Tori racing to a new hiding place, It may call, "One-two-three on Tori" and race her back to Base to imprison her again.

But whenever It finds Tori, if Tori reaches Home Base first, not only is she safe but also any other imprisoned players are freed.

The first person to be captured three times becomes the new It, and the game starts over.

16

Beep!

If you've ever played Buzz (page 29), you already have the general idea behind this game. But in Beep! it's letters, not numbers, that you avoid saying aloud, substituting the name of the game for them. Specifically, the letters you don't want to say aloud are vowels. In Beep! you're required to spell words, but every time you come to a vowel, you have to say "Beep!" instead.

For comic effect, you can beep like the Roadrunner, like an old auto, like an answering machine, or in any funny way you want, though this isn't required.

If Jon and Pete are playing, Jon might say, "Magazine."

Pete now must spell the word as follows: M - Beep! - G - Beep! - Z - Beep! - N - Beep!" If he fails to beep when he's supposed to or inserts a beep! where it's not needed—or if he misspells the word in any other way—he's out of the game. If he genuinely doesn't know how to spell the word, he can request another word, however. This isn't a spelling bee.

T W O
or more

MATERIALS

✐ None

17

O N E
or more

MATERIALS

✐ None

Beyond Pig Latin

Pig Latin is the best known of the "secret languages" of childhood, though there are many others that have been invented over the years. Many involve the insertion of a sound or syllable into every word or even every syllable in order to confuse unauthorized listeners.

Can your child invent a new secret language? How will it work? What are the rules for speaking this new "language," and for deciphering it when you hear it?

The next time she has free time—after school or otherwise—let her spend some of the time inventing a new secret language.

Big Talkers

Every player gets a turn looking in the dictionary. He should choose a big word—one he really doubts the other players know—and he should make sure he understands the meaning after reading it in the dictionary. Then he thinks of a sentence using that word and writes the sentence down, to be sure he doesn't forget it. He can choose a sentence that uses the word correctly, or he can choose a sentence that uses it very wrongly.

    Then each player takes a turn reading his sentence aloud. The other players have to decide whether the player has used the word correctly or wrongly. For every player you fool, you get a point. (If you've used the word correctly and an opponent says you've used it wrongly, or if you've purposely used the word wrongly and your opponent says you've used it rightly, either way you get a point.) A round consists of each player using one word. A game consists of five rounds. At the end of the game, the player who has the most points is the winner.

T W O
or more
(and the more, the merrier)

MATERIALS

✐ Dictionary (preferably but not necessarily unabridged), paper, pen or pencil

Big-Circle Beanbag

MATERIALS

✍ One beanbag per player

Here's a game with no winners, no losers, and no scoring. This is best played outdoors, as you need an area large enough that the players can stand in a circle with at least 3 or 4 feet between each player.

The game starts with everyone using an underhand toss—the rule throughout the game—to propel his beanbag to the player across from him. As a player catches a beanbag, he immediately throws it to someone else . . . anyone except his immediate neighbors. Optionally, a rule can be established that players should call out the names of the players they're throwing to. In a group of any appreciable number, though, each name will likely be drowned out by all the others.

If a beanbag falls in front of a player, he must bend down to retrieve it at the earliest safe opportunity . . . but he'd better beware of flying beanbags as he stands up again!

At some point, either throwing arms will tire, or players will laugh so hard they collapse in a heap on the floor, or the fun might just begin to wane. At that point, it's time to end the game.

Biking to Disney World®

If you're concerned that your child's activities after school are too much of the sedentary variety, here's a way to encourage him to get out and get a little exercise: Promise him (yes, the word is "bribe") a treat when he has biked or walked a certain distance.

The treat may be directly connected to the distance: "When you have biked the equivalent of the distance from here to Disney World, we'll actually take a vacation there." The connection may be a little less specific: "When you have walked 25 miles, we'll go to the arcade and give you $10 in spending money."

Or, in a multi-child family, you can turn it into a competition: "Between Monday and Friday whoever bikes/walks the farthest distance is excused from chores this weekend."

If you're trying to cover the equivalent of the distance between home and a certain destination (e.g., Disney World, Grandma's house in Dubuque), you can mark a map every night in highlighter, showing the distance the child has biked that day and how far toward the goal destination he has gotten.

MATERIALS

- Bike or exercise bike with odometer, or pedometer (to measure walking distance)

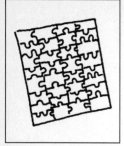

Blank Jigsaw Puzzles

MATERIALS

✎ Cardboard, scissors, pencil with eraser, paint

Your child can make a jigsaw puzzle that will be particularly challenging to solve, even for her after creating it herself. Why? There's no picture to guide her in putting it together! That's right—it's a blank jigsaw puzzle. And she'll have double fun with it—first creating it, then putting it together again. Here's how to create it:

In pencil, lightly draw cut lines on one side. Whether your puzzle has five pieces, twenty-five, fifty, or two hundred will depend on your child's age and ability to solve jigsaw puzzles. Erase any lines you're not pleased with.

Paint the other side of the cardboard. (This step can be eliminated if your cardboard is already two different colors on the two sides. The sole purpose in painting it is so that your child—and any friend who plays with the puzzle—knows which side goes up. Otherwise the puzzle becomes impossible to solve.)

When the paint is dry, cut along the cut lines.

Scramble the pieces and try to reassemble them. (It isn't easy, even though you created the puzzle, is it?)

22

Blottos

Fold various pieces of paper down the middle and open them again. Then sprinkle a few drops of paint (either all the same color or two or three different colors) on one side of each piece of paper, near the fold.

Now fold each piece of paper on the crease, then open again. You should have a symmetrical and interesting design on each sheet of paper.

If you wish, you can cut the designs out and glue the cutouts to a sheet of white or (for more dramatic effect) black construction paper

O N E

MATERIALS

✐ Paper, watercolor paint or thin tempera paint

✂ Optional: Black or white construction paper, glue, scissors

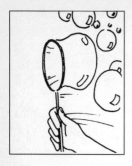

Blow Soap Bubbles

Safety reminder:
Liquid detergent can
be harmful if ingested.

MATERIALS

- 1/2 cup of liquid detergent, 3/4 gallon of water, 2 tablespoons glycerine, bowl

- Optional: Eyeglass frames with a lens missing or paper clip or wire hanger

You don't need to spend money on expensive commercial bubble preparations. Mix the ingredients listed at the side in a bowl, and presto! You have a bubble solution.

You don't need an expensive bubble wand either. Just make a circle of your thumb and forefinger, then dip it into the solution and either wave your hand gently through the air or blow softly into the glistening soap film that stretches across your encircling fingers. As an alternative, you can bend a paper clip into a circle and use that as a bubble wand, or you can use an old pair of eyeglass frames with one or both lenses missing, or blow giant bubbles through a wire hanger that you've stretched into a more circular shape than its normal quasi-triangle.

Bottle-Cap Basketball

The name of the game describes it: Players attempt to sink baskets by throwing bottle caps at an empty wastebasket from a reasonably challenging distance.

Two or more players can turn it into a competition. Each has ten bottle caps (or five, or seven, according to what's available) and tries to sink the largest possible number. Too easy? Move the wastebasket, or stand farther back. The winner, of course, is the player who sinks the most baskets.

A solo player can have fun, too. First see how many baskets you can sink out of ten tries; then try to do better on each successive round.

Try some trick shots: "blind" shots with your eyes closed; backward shots, thrown over your head; overhand rather than underhand. (Before trying any trick play that might result in some wild throws that could hit lamps, windows, and so forth, consider taking the game outdoors, or at least to a basement or other low-risk area.)

ONE
or more

MATERIALS

✐ Empty wastebasket, bottle caps

Boxed In

O N E
or more

MATERIALS

Cardboard box

In these days of hi-tech toys, parents often overlook the pleasures to be found in the simplest of toys and items-not-originally-intended-as-toys—like boxes. The bigger, the better; but even small boxes are fun, if they're big enough to get both feet into.

The younger ones can have fun with a box just large enough to put their feet into. Suddenly they're standing in a tippy canoe . . . or on board a raft . . . or . . . Put even some twelve-year-olds in a refrigerator carton, and they're in a spaceship to the moon, a submarine chasing after underwater volcanoes, or a cave full of mystery.

What's more, if you give your child a handful of markers and turn him loose inside a large appliance carton, he can have another afternoon's worth of fun drawing the inside of whatever-the-box-is. Is it a schoolroom? If so, he can draw the blackboard, the bulletin board, the window, and its view of freedom beyond. Is it a submarine? If so, he can draw the control panel. Whatever it is, he can draw the appropriate scene.

26

Braided Heart

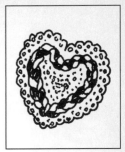

Hearts are always appropriate. Though this decoration is especially suited to Valentine's Day, I myself have a handmade heart decoration, although of a different sort, which my daughter made for me, hanging on my wall permanently from season to season. Here's how your child can create a braided heart:

Glue one end of each of the three lengths of yarn together and braid the three colors together. When you're done braiding, glue the other ends of the three colors together. You now have a single braid; glue the two ends of this braid together to form a circle, and leave it to dry.

Spread glue on one side of this braided circle and, with this glued side facing down, form it into a heart shape on the doily. You now have a braided heart. Press it down onto the doily to anchor it in place.

O N E

MATERIALS

✐ 12-inch lengths of red, white, and pink yarn; large white paper lace doily; glue

Button Box Fun

MATERIALS

✐ Mom's button box; any of the following: a compartmentalized plastic box or egg carton, cardboard or construction paper; needle and thread

There's loads of fun to be had in a button box. When I was a child, I used to love to paw through the rich assortment of buttons in my mom's button box, reorganizing the order in which she kept them. Just playing with the buttons, feeling the textures, and admiring the fancy kinds can fill a good chunk of an afternoon.

If your button box is less organized than mine is and my mom's was, your child can have fun organizing it. If your button box isn't compartmentalized, consider letting your child organize your buttons in one or more egg cartons, where you may even want to leave them.

There are many ways to separate and organize buttons, such as by the number of holes, by the size, by the color, and by whether they're strictly practical or ornamental.

When your child is through organizing them, if she's old enough to use a needle responsibly, she can sew extra buttons to paper or cardboard to create designs. Flowers, faces, dogs, clocks, and many other forms, not to mention abstract designs, are among the possibilities for button pictures.

Buzz

Buzz is a counting game, an elimination game, and a fun game. In it, players count from one up, but any time a player's turn would require him to say either a number that contains a 7 in it (e.g., 17) or a number that's a multiple of 7 (e.g., 49), he mustn't say it . . . or he's out of the game. Instead, he says "Buzz." Failing to "Buzz" when needed—or saying "Buzz" when you shouldn't—will get you out of the game. Last player left is the winner.

The first player says "One." The second says "Two." The third (or the first again in a two-player game) says "Three," and so on. Here's how it should sound, counting as far as 22: 1 - 2 - 3 - 4 - 5 - 6 - BUZZ - 8 - 9 - 10 - 11 - 12 - 13 - BUZZ - 15 - 16 - BUZZ - 18 - 19 - 20 - BUZZ - 22 . . . got the idea?

T W O
or more

MATERIALS

✐ None

29

100, 97,
94, 91,
88, 85,
82, 79,
76, 73,

By Threes . . .
Backward

O N E

MATERIALS

✎ None

Can you count backward—100 - 99 - 98 - 97 - and so on? Can you count by threes—3 - 6 - 9 - 12 - and so on? Can you count backward by threes? Start at 100, and try: 100 - 97 - 94 - 91 . . . If you get all the way down, try again . . . starting at 99 this time: 99 - 96 - 93 - 90 - and so on. Now you can try it starting at 98.

If all this seems too easy, give yourself some other challenges. For example, count backward by sevens, or starting at 500 . . . or both! Can you count backward by sevens from 500?

A Calendar Just for Fun

Do you wish the weekends were longer? Why not invent a calendar that matches all your wishes?! Of course you can't make the week really be like that . . . but it's still fun to dream!

How many days are there going to be in your week? How about an eight-day week with four weekdays and four weekend days? Do you hate Mondays? Rename the first day of the week! What will you call it? Funday?

Once you've decided how many days there will be in your week, lay out a grid on your piece of paper, with as many squares going across as there are days in your week and as many squares going down as there are weeks in your month. Now name your days. Of course, you can use the traditional names, with two Saturdays and two Sundays if you want a nine-day week, for example, but how about giving your days new names? Why not name one of the days after yourself? What will your other days be named?

Just remember that when Monday on the regular calendar rolls around, you still have to go to school . . . no matter what your calendar says!

ONE
or more

MATERIALS

Blank paper, marking pen, ruler

31

A Calendar of Your Child's Own

MATERIALS

✐ Thirteen sheets of white construction paper, fine-line markers, hole punch, loose-leaf rings or twist ties or yarn

✂ Optional: Photos, magazine pictures, glue, scissors

Your child can make a calendar of his very own, complete with pictures. First draw a grid of five (or in a few cases, six) squares down by seven across. Consulting another calendar will show what day of the week the first of each month falls on and will help if the old rhyme isn't enough to remind him which months have how many days.

He'll need to lay out twelve such grids, each on a sheet of white construction paper. He'll also need a cover page on which he can write the year; the back of that page holds the picture for January.

Be sure the pages are right-side up in the right order. Punch two holes at the top of each page and hook them together with loose-leaf rings, twist ties, or yarn. Punch a hole in the center of the bottom of each page for hanging the calendar.

Now flip each page over and decorate it by one of the following methods: Draw a picture on it; glue a photo on it; glue a magazine picture on it.

The last step is to mark all important dates on the calendar: school holidays, birthdays of family and friends, and any other important occasions.

Candy 'n' Cake

The most fun in this activity is in decorating the cake, though baking it is certainly fun too. So if your child isn't old enough to bake alone, or at all, that doesn't disqualify him from taking part in this activity. It just means you, the parent, have to bake the cake yourself first or help him to bake it. Then he can take over with the decorating. Here's what it's all about:

Bake a cake and frost it with a can of frosting (or with frosting made from scratch, if you prefer). Then break out the candy and get ready to have fun.

How are you going to decorate the cake? You can use the small candies to draw a picture, create a face, or even spell a word or name. If it's a birthday cake, spell out HAPPY BIRTHDAY in candies or spell out the birthday child's name. If it's the second Sunday in May, and the cake is for Mom, spell out HAPPY MOTHER'S DAY. Draw the outlines of stars, a crescent moon, or even a car.

That cake's going to look so nice, it'll be a shame to cut into it and ruin the design! But you will . . . I have confidence in that! Cakes are not just for looking at!

ONE

with parental help as appropriate in use of the oven

MATERIALS

✎ Box of cake mix, other ingredients called for on box, cake pan of size and shape called for on box, can of instant frosting, large bag of M&Ms or Reese's Pieces or Hershey's Kisses (or a combination of some or all of these candies)

33

A Carton of Fun—1

O N E
or more

MATERIALS

Empty, washed
1-quart milk
cartons

There are various ways in which empty, washed quart milk cartons can hold lots more than a quart of fun. Here's two:

You can substitute milk cartons for the tp tubes suggested in T-P Bowling (page 330) or the dominoes in Domino Knockdown (page 64). Set up ten cartons either in a row or in the standard bowling-pin arrangement, and roll a tennis ball at them to see if you can knock them down. There is one ball per frame, not two.

You can fill the cartons about a third with sand or dirt or gravel, and place them on a fence, a milk crate, or a sturdy box. Throw a tennis ball or a dirt clod (or a rock, if there's absolutely no danger of hitting another person) at the milk cartons, trying to knock each one over with one throw.

A Carton of Fun—2

Here's a variation on the bowling-at-milk-cartons idea. After washing out the cartons and drying the outsides, mark a number between 1 and 10 on the sides of each carton. These are point values. Each milk carton should have a different point value, which should be repeated on each of the four sides of the carton.

Your child now sets up the cartons in a random arrangement, not bowling-pin fashion, with the cartons close but not touching, and rolls a tennis ball across the lawn or patio at the cartons. She scores the total point value of all the cartons she knocks over. On each successive roll, she can try to better her previous score, or she can simply try to do her best on each roll.

Alternative: You, the parent, mark the point value on one side only of each carton, and you set the cartons up in a different configuration each time. You face the marked side away from your child, so she is uninformed as to the value of any given carton till she has rolled the ball and knocked over the cartons; then she tallies up her score.

O N E

MATERIALS

Empty, washed 1-quart milk cartons; marking pen; tennis ball

35

A Carton of Fun—3

MATERIALS

- Empty, washed quart or half-gallon milk cartons

Younger kids, too, can have fun with milk cartons. Once emptied and washed, they make great boats, locomotives, pickup trucks, or other vehicles. The boats are particularly fun, since they behave in a tub or wading pool the way they're supposed to, floating, gliding, and sinking when scuttled, while "wheeled" vehicles only slide, which requires a little more imagination.

The child most likely to be amused in this way is one too young to be wielding sharp scissors or knives, so parental help is needed in cutting the milk cartons into boats, trucks, or whatever. X-acto knives or linoleum knives are particularly useful here. Once you've done the cutting, though, your child is on his own. Although cartons tend to be pretty heavily decorated already, some kids like to use paint or markers to color the outside of the vehicles. But that isn't necessary—the only thing really essential is a good imagination.

Catch My Act!

You've probably been to the circus, and you probably loved the tightrope walkers. You can be a junior tightrope walker yourself . . . without ever leaving the safety of the ground.

If there's a sidewalk on your street, and if it's composed of two squares side by side, there's a long crack running up the street between the two squares. Can you walk along the crack without losing your balance and "falling off"?

If there's no sidewalk on your street, stretch a loooooooong piece of string out in your yard, and walk the string from one end to the other without a misstep.

Next week you can try being a clown!

O N E

MATERIALS

✐ The crack between sidewalk segments or a string stretched out in your yard

37

Checker Chase

MATERIALS

Ten checkers, shoe box, scissors

First prepare the shoe box: After discarding the lid, cut a hole in the middle of the top of one end of the box. The hole should be a little taller than a checker that's standing on its end, and about an inch wide. Cut a similar hole at the other end; this hole should be about 2 inches wide.

To play, place the shoe box upside down on a smooth surface. The holes should be touching the surface, with the smaller hole facing you. If playing on a tabletop, place the shoe box about a foot away from the edge. If playing on a floor, position yourself about a foot from the box.

Place one checker at a time on its side, rolling it at the smaller hole. If it goes in, score 5 points; if it comes out again at the other end, score another 10 points. When you've rolled all ten checkers, add up your score.

If playing against another player, one of you rolls red checkers and one of you rolls black. For solo play, try to beat your previous best score.

If you suspect checkers are building up inside the box and blocking the progress of other checkers, stop the game long enough to remove the accumulated checkers.

Checker Roll

On the sidewalk (or in the street, if you live in a sidewalk-less, traffic-safe cul de sac), draw in chalk four circles in a straight line, with each circle farther away from you than the one before. Each circle should be larger than a checker, and there should be one checker's width between each circle and the next. Write the point value for each circle within it: The nearest circle is 10, the next circle 30, the next one 5, and the last one 25. About a foot back from the nearest circle, draw a lag line, which players will stand behind to roll the checkers at the circles.

The first player starts and rolls a checker from behind the lag line, aiming at the circles. If any part of the checker lands at all within a circle, she gets credit for the point value of that circle. Then the next player picks up the checker and rolls. Players continue alternating till each player has had ten turns. The player with the highest score wins.

T W O
or more

MATERIALS

✏ Chalk, checker

39

Chests to Treasure

MATERIALS

Hinged-top
wooden box, paint
and paintbrush

It's always neat to get your hands on something ordinary and turn it into something extraordinary. Your child can get much of this kind of pleasure if he buys a small, hinged-top wooden box, available in a hobby or crafts store, and paints a pretty picture or design on the box.

He can decorate just the lid or cover the entire box with a design. Go for a traditional theme—a flower, a sunset, a sweeping landscape, or a graceful tree—or paint an abstract design or a pattern of swirling colors.

Though oil paint works great for this project, this isn't the place to start becoming familiar with the medium for the first time. If your child isn't already comfortable working with oil paints, he can achieve fine results with acrylic paints or tempera.

He can happily turn a plain pine box into a favorite toy, a treasure . . . maybe even an heirloom.

Chinese-Style Screen

What with the need to use a linoleum knife or similarly effective cutting tool, this is definitely a project that calls for parental involvement. Your part: Remove the top, the bottom, and one side of a large appliance carton. The remaining three sides, unfolded slightly, should stand up on their own. If they don't, cut makeshift feet out of the discarded cardboard and attach them with duct tape to the stand-up part.

Now comes your child's part in this project: Decorate the screen. Use markers (either broad or fine-line) or paint to paint anything from a solid color to a scenic panorama, people, animals, or even a geometric pattern. As an alternative, he can cover the screen with wallpaper scraps, pieces of fabric, pictures cut from magazines, whole comic strips, or individual characters cut out from the comics. There are two sides to this pretty large screen—decorating it ought to keep him busy for a while . . . maybe even several days.

O N E
and parent

MATERIALS

- Large appliance carton, linoleum knife or similar cutting tool (to be used by parent!), markers or paints and paintbrush

- Optional: Duct tape

Clay Miniatures

MATERIALS

✐ Modeling clay

✂ Optional: Oven

How would your daughter like a teacup set for her dollhouse, a tiny vase for her bookcase, or even a miniature sculpture? How would your son like a scale-model club for his caveman action figure? How would he like a set of dinosaurs he fashioned himself? How about a cowboy to sit upon his toy horse . . . or a horse for his cowboy to sit on?

It's all possible with nonstaining modeling clay, available at your local hobby or crafts shop. You have a choice of self-hardening clay, which dries in a few hours, or clay that remains pliable till exposed to heat (usually a few minutes in a moderate oven), or clay that remains pliant forever.

Making miniatures is a very absorbing hobby that can carry over into adulthood. Yet it fascinates the heck out of kids, too.

Your hobby shop will be glad to answer any questions you have about the handling of the particular clay you've bought.

Clock Solitaire

Place one card in each of the twelve positions of the numbers on an old-fashioned clock face and one card in the center of the circle, then repeat three more times till all cards have been dealt. The Ace pile is the pile where the 1 would be on the clock face, the deuce pile is at the two o'clock position, and so on. The Jack pile is eleven o'clock, the Queen pile is in the twelve o'clock position, and the King pile goes in the center. You're ready to play.

ONE

MATERIALS

✎ Deck of cards (bridge/poker, not pinochle)

Take the top card from the King pile and turn it faceup, placing it under the pile to which it belongs. (For instance, if it's a 9, place it under the pile of cards in the nine o'clock position.) Now take a card from the top of the pile under which you just placed the faceup card (the nine pile, in this case), and turn it faceup. Place it under the appropriate pile, taking the top card from that pile in turn, and so on.

The game continues until all four Kings have been turned faceup. If the fourth King comes up while there are still other cards turned facedown, you lose. But if you uncover everything else before you turn the last King, then you win.

43

Clown Wall Hanging

MATERIALS

- One piece of burlap approximately 2 by 3 feet, bright-colored rickrack, buttons, felt, glue, needle, and thread

- Optional: Scraps of fake fur

You're never too old for the circus. (Ask any grandmother who adores bringing her grandkids to the circus every year, as mine did.) And no kid is too old to have a clown-themed wall hanging in his room. Kids old enough to use a needle responsibly can make their own clown wall hanging, by following these instructions:

Divide one side of the burlap into sections, using the rickrack as a divider and gluing it into place. There's no hard-and-fast rule about the size of the sections, but a 2-by-3-foot piece of burlap would give you six 1-by-1-foot sections, which would work well.

Within each section, create a clown's face. Here's how: Sew buttons on for the eyes, and either use a smaller one for the nose or glue pieces of felt or fake fur on for the nose. Felt or fur will also create a mouth and make good hair, as well, if you want.

Optional touches include hats made of felt, red cheeks made of circles of red felt, and a rickrack border all around the edges of the burlap.

Coded Messages "By the Book"

Here's a mysterious way to create a secret message. This is complex and definitely only for older kids!

The key to the code is a book. Pick any book—that's why this code is impossible to break. Both parties must know what the book is to encode and decode the message.

The code consists of groups of four numbers. Suppose the sender wants to encode the name DAVID, for example. And suppose he and his partner-in-mystery have agreed that their key is the Dell Island paperback edition of John Grisham's *The Partner*. Here's how he'd encode the name DAVID: 398 1 6 5 52 1 1 1 142 21 5 1 1 2 3 1 1 17 12 1

Each letter is represented by four numbers. The first number is the page number of the key book. The second number refers to the number of the line on that page. The third digit points to a word in that line—word number two, number six, and so forth. The fourth digit finally gives us the letter itself. If you look on page 398 of *The Partner*, and find line one, the sixth word in that line (GRAND), and the fifth letter . . . yep, it's D.

O N E

MATERIALS

✐ Paper, pencil

Collage Box

MATERIALS

Magazine pictures, scissors, glue, container such as shoe box or cigar box

One way to encourage your child to keep his room neat is to provide him with containers for his myriad baseball cards, miniature soldiers, marbles, and other small items. And what better encouragement than to have him create the containers himself:

Start with a box. This could be a shoe box, a cigar box, or anything else along those lines. Cut appealing pictures from magazines. It's best if you follow a theme, for example, all pictures of cars, all pictures of animals, or flowers, or some other theme. Don't cut out a square within which is a picture of a fire engine; cut right around the fire engine itself.

When you've assembled a variety of whatever subject you've selected, glue the pictures in place on the box. Since the nature of a collage calls for the various pictures to overlap and a certain amount of artfulness is called for, you'll probably want to put the pictures down dry first. Rearrange them and play with the positioning before you commit to gluing them in place.

Finished? Great! Now you have a box for your baseball cards. How about another for your marbles, and another for . . .

Collect Odd Facts

Did you know that giraffes, despite having such long necks, have no vocal cords? That's right—those long-necked giraffes can't talk. Do you know what the most popular, most common first name in the world is? It's not the very-common JOHN, or its translations in various languages—JUAN, JEAN, and so on. It's MUHAMMAD.

More odd facts:

- No word in the English language rhymes with MONTH, ORANGE, SILVER, or PURPLE.
- DREAMT is the only English word that ends in the letters "mt."
- All fifty states are listed across the top of the Lincoln Memorial on the back of the $5 bill.
- Maine is the only state whose name is just one syllable.

Start a collection of odd facts like these. You can even turn it into a homemade "book."

O N E

MATERIALS

✐ Encyclopedia and/or other books and/or magazines, paper, pen or pencil

47

Comical Books 1—
Words First

MATERIALS

✎ Paper, pen or pencil, magazines, scissors, glue

A bit of gentle ribbing between family members is the order of the day when Comical Books are the activity du jour. There are two ways to go about creating Comical Books. Here's the words-first method:

One child writes a brief story (true or otherwise) about herself. She writes it on several pages, leaving ample room for illustrations. Then she passes the pages to another child. He, in turn, seeks illustrations for those words among the magazines spread out in front of him . . . but the illustrations don't exactly bear up the words in the story.

For instance, if Gina wrote, "And then I got into my shiny new car," Brian might now cut out, and paste onto the page, a picture of a terrible old jalopy, or a truck that's been in a wreck, or an Army jeep.

Of course, while Brian is making hash out of Gina's story, she's similarly seeking illustrations to show her version of his story!

48

Comical Books 2—
Pictures First

In this version of Comical Books, the pictures come first and then the story. This involves each child cutting out pictures and pasting them down on several pages, then passing them to a sibling, who writes a story to go with the pictures. As with the Words First version of Comical Books, the story is about the other sibling.

A picture of a clown might elicit words about Lisa's cute new boyfriend. An illustration of a rhinoceros might inspire words about Lou's new horse. Just remember, it's all in fun!

T W O
or more

MATERIALS

✐ Paper, pen or pencil, magazines, scissors, glue

Complete-a-Story

O N E
or more, with parent

MATERIALS

✐ Book

✂ Optional: Paper,
   pen or pencil

This is a cooperative effort; it involves at least a minimal amount of time on your part. It also involves a book your child has not yet read and doesn't know the ending of. You start in one of three ways:

- Read your child a part of a story or book.
- Summarize for your child the plot of part of a story or book.
- Mark a point in a book, put your child on his honor, and tell him to read up to that point and then stop.

The point at which you stop reading or telling the story should be some sort of cliff-hanger point at which the major situation or problem depicted in the book has not yet been resolved.

From there, it's up to your child to complete the story. He can write his ending down or simply tell it to you. After he completes the story his way, it's fun to compare his ending to the original. (Don't refer to the original as the "right" ending—it's important he not be made to feel anything else is a "wrong" ending. It's the original ending and his ending.)

Control Panel

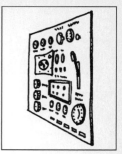

Ever wish you could change the world? Ever wish that in the same way you turn the knobs to control the TV, you could turn a knob and change the way things are around you? If you could, what would you change? Would you adjust the amount of homework, make your parents less strict . . . or what?

Design a control panel for the world. It won't really work, of course, but it'll be a lot of fun wishing and pretending. You can draw knobs, levers, push buttons, or some other arrangement. You can have them control bedtime, schoolwork, people, events . . . you're the boss!

Ready, set . . . draw!

O N E

MATERIALS

✏ Large piece of cardboard (preferably a big piece such as might be cut from the side of a carton, though an ordinary piece of 8½-by-11-inch cardboard, or even paper, will do in a pinch), marking pen

Crab Soccer

MATERIALS

One ball (soccer ball, playground ball, basketball, tennis ball, or rubber ball), something to delineate goals (e.g., two boxes, or anything with which to mark two goals)

Crab Soccer can be played indoors or out. The aim of the game, as in regular soccer, is to propel the ball into the goal, which can be the space between two boxes laid on their sides, the space between two sneakers, or the area under the ping-pong table. But regular soccer was never played in this position! All play is accomplished in the "crab" position! That is, players remain at all times on their hands and feet, with the face and torso turned upward.

If you play outdoors, the ball can be a soccer ball, basketball, or playground ball; for indoor play, a tennis ball or rubber ball is better. You can play individually, two players can compete against each other, or teams of anywhere up to a dozen or even more can play against each other.

The rules are simple: Players must maintain the crab position and may only propel the ball with their feet. Any additional rules that players wish to impose, regarding fouls or offsides or out-of-bounds, are optional.

Crayon-Stub Stained Glass

Parental help is called for with this activity, which requires the use of both a grater and an iron. Start by peeling the labels off a bunch of crayon stubs you've saved up. You mainly want bright colors here.

Turn your iron on to the low setting (dry, not steam), and let it warm up. Meanwhile, put down several thicknesses of newspaper and, above that, a piece of waxed paper, perhaps a foot square. Now sprinkle the crayon gratings down on the waxed paper, intermixing the colors. Don't clump the gratings too thickly. Spread another piece of waxed paper, the same size, on top of the crayon gratings.

Run the iron lightly across the top square of waxed paper till all the gratings have melted and run together. Your "stained glass" window decoration is ready to be hung.

Optional: Create a pleasing design of cutouts in a sheet of black construction paper and mount it in front of the waxed-paper "stained glass." The colors will show through the cutout pattern.

ONE
with parental help in use
of grater and iron

MATERIALS

✐ Crayon stubs, grater, iron, waxed paper, newspaper, tape (such as Scotch Tape)

✂ Optional: Black construction paper

53

Create a Board Game

You enjoy board games—why not create one?!

Draw the game board on a large piece of poster board or cardboard. Lay out the path, with a START/HOME square and various other squares. Now think of a theme. It could be sports, knights-and-dragons, the West, race cars, or even school.

Some of your squares will be neutral—nothing special happens when you land on them. Others should have hazards or rewards. For a knights-and-dragons game, a square might be marked MEET DRAGON IN WOODS, BACK FIVE SPACES or KNIGHT RESCUES PRINCESS, AHEAD FOUR SPACES. Other rewards and penalties might be TRADE PLACES WITH ANY OTHER PLAYER or TAKE EXTRA TURN.

Some squares can require you to pick index cards from a deck. These can say more of the same sort of thing or require you to do something, like repeat a tongue twister successfully, in order to advance extra squares.

Use coins, nuts, paper clips, or playing pieces from other games as your playing pieces to move around the board.

Create a Cityscape

Your child can make a city landscape using food boxes and either poster board or one side of a large carton. The boxes will be the buildings. A spaghetti container, standing on end, can be a skyscraper; another, on its side, might be an airport terminal, a school, or a garden apartment building.

This is a project slated to take more than one afternoon, or perhaps a long day over a weekend or school holiday. Here's how to do it:

Paint the "buildings" a suitable color, covering the printing on the box in the process. Use silver to paint on windows, or if the box has a plastic see-through "window" (such as a spaghetti box has), paint lines across it to divide it into several smaller windows for the building.

Decide where you're going to place the buildings, then paint roads, sidewalks, parks, and other features onto the poster board or cardboard. Finally glue the buildings down onto the base.

If you have any small action figures or dolls, they can populate the city. Otherwise, you can draw little people on construction paper and cut them out if you want to.

O N E

MATERIALS

Empty food boxes of various sizes and shapes (e.g., spaghetti boxes, oatmeal containers, rice boxes), glue, large piece of poster board or one side of a large carton, paints and paintbrush

Create a Garland

MATERIALS

Scissors
(beginner's
scissors
are okay),
construction
paper, tape or
glue or stapler

Your child can create garlands out of colored construction paper and festoon his room—or the family room, or the dinette—with these colorful decorations. Here's how to make one:

Cut two equal-sized strips of construction paper, as long as you can get out of one sheet and perhaps 1½ inches wide each. Choose two colors that complement each other and match or complement the room they're to go in. Place one end of each of the two strips across the other so that the two form a right angle, or L shape, and attach them together with glue, tape, or a stapler.

Let's assume the two colors are blue and violet, and you've pasted the blue strip above the violet strip. Fold the violet strip over the blue strip and press down tightly on the fold. Now fold the blue strip over the violet strip and press down on the fold again. Continue flapping each strip over the other and pressing down on the crease.

When you get to the two ends, glue or staple or tape them together, and gently pull the garland out—not so hard that it tears. Now you can hang the garland . . . or attach it to the end of another garland to make one long one before hanging it.

Create a Rebus

Though your child will want to show her friends any rebus she creates, to see if they can figure it out, creating these puzzles is a solo effort. A pair or group of friends (or siblings) can each create a rebus, then trade and see if each can figure out the other's puzzle. A child working alone can happily bring the completed rebus to school the next day to show friends.

ONE
or more

MATERIALS

✎ Paper, pen or pencil

Most kids are familiar with deciphering the rebus form by the time they're seven or eight. In a rebus, a letter, number, or simple drawing represents a word. Thus, a picture of an eye precedes the word LOVE and a U to spell out I LOVE YOU. The word FORTUNATE is spelled "4tune8" or even "4 2 n 8," and a whole sentence can be written "I am 4 2n8 2 no U." Or substitute a picture of an eye for the first I. SEE YOU LATER is "C U l8r."

How many rebus puzzles can your child create?

57

Critters

MATERIALS

✐ Paper, crayons

What would you call an animal with the head of an ostrich, the fur of a kitten, the feet of a hippo, the wings of an eagle, the curly tail of a pig, and the . . . ? What other odd combinations can you come up with?

Your child can have fun dreaming up animals the likes of which have never been seen on this earth. He can simply draw them and name them, or if he's really into it, he can also give further descriptions, including specifying what animals it's a cross between.

He can have further fun by imagining critters that are crosses between animals and inanimate objects—a lion whose mane wafts away when blown like the white fuzz of a dandelion, a dodo with a helicopter-style rotor growing out of its head to help it fly.

(You may want to explain to your child that you can't really cross a llama with a yak, or a giraffe with a seal. He probably already knows that you can't really cross a hippopotamus with a tree so that the branches offer the animal shade in the heat of an African day. But he can still have fun drawing one.)

Custom-Designed Jewelry

To make a striking and unique necklace, you'll need clay you can get from a hobby shop—this can be either the self-hardening kind or the kind that remains soft till it's baked briefly in the oven.

The procedure here is to make small beads or coin-shaped medallions, of a size appropriate to a necklace. Once the beads or disks have been formed, you can decorate the still-soft clay by pressing any of various items into it to leave an impression that will decorate the finished bead or medallion. Some suggestions include lace, a pine branch, a coin, a leaf, or even repeated impressions of a nail head.

Make a hole in each piece with either a small knitting needle or a large nail, then thread the dental floss through the individual beads or medallions, using an ordinary sewing needle.

ᛏ
O N E
or more

MATERIALS

✐ Clay, dental floss, sewing needle, knitting needle or nail

✂ Optional: Lace, pine branch, coin, leaf, nail head, oven

Design a Flag for Your Hometown

ONE

The United States has a flag. Your state has a flag, even if you're not familiar with it. But does your town or city have a flag? Would you like to design one? Chances are the mayor won't proclaim your flag to be the town's new official flag . . . but don't let that stop you from the fun of designing one anyhow.

You can use stripes, stars, large dots, zigzags, a checkered pattern, areas of solid color, swirls . . . you're the one who's designing it. Now—what's your town well known for? Does it have lots of pine tress or palm trees? Draw a pine tree or palm tree on the flag. Lots of factories? Draw smokestacks. A wonderful beach? Draw the ocean. A wild woods? Draw a group of trees.

What else can you draw flags for? Your school? Your Scout troop? Your gymnastics class? Your school band? Your summer camp?

Design and Name a Car

Suppose you could design a car. What would it look like? Draw the outside of it. Draw the dashboard, too, if you'd like.

What would you name your car? Names are important. An attractive name sells cars.

While you're at it, why not design some other vehicles? How about a car with a rotor (propeller) on top, like a helicopter has? If you get stuck in a traffic jam, start up the rotor and just fly straight up out of the traffic! What would you call such a vehicle? A helicar? An automocopter? And what would the brand name and model name be?

O N E

MATERIALS

✐ Paper, pencil with eraser

Designer Lunch Bags

O N E

That same old PBJ will taste better if it's carried in a jauntily decorated lunch bag. You can easily spruce up tomorrow's lunch bag—or several days' worth at once—in any of several ways:

MATERIALS

⊘ Brown paper
lunch bags,
markers or
crayons, scissors,
color comic
strips, glue

- Draw a design—or several of them—on the lunch bag.
- Write your name on the bag, or write a funny saying such as TOP SECRET: JEFF'S LUNCH.
- Cut out color comics and paste them on the bag. Either cut out one whole strip or several people or animals from different strips (e.g., Garfield and Snoopy in a couple of poses each).

I advise against using glitter in decorating the bag; some of it can get onto your hands and work its way into your lunch.

Do Play with Your Food!

No, I'm not encouraging you to make castles out of your mashed potatoes or have a food fight! But there's no reason you can't have a little fun with your food . . . by drawing faces on your sandwich!

Jazz up an open-faced sandwich by adding to it the features of a face. Use such items as olives (or olive slices), radish slices, carrot slices, or similar round food for eyes and a nose; a pickle strip or strip of green pepper (or red bell pepper) for a mouth, and possibly pickle slices for ears and carrot curls for hair.

You can even use strips and slices of banana to draw a face on a peanut butter sandwich.

O N E
or more

with parental help
when using the knife

MATERIALS

✐ Open-faced sandwich (e.g., tuna salad, chicken salad, grilled cheese); knife; decorations such as olives, pickle slices or strips, small pieces of carrot or celery, green pepper strips, pimiento strips, and radish slices

63

Domino Knockdown

MATERIALS

Set of dominoes, marble

Looking for another solo challenge that can also be played competitively? Look no farther than your box of dominoes . . . and set 'em up with ten in a straight line, as follows: On a flat surface (e.g., wood floor, smooth vinyl tile, or linoleum), set up one domino so that it stands on end with the broad side facing you. About ¾ inch behind it, set up another domino in the same manner, and continue till you have ten of them set up in a straight line that gets progressively farther away.

Now stand (or kneel, or crouch) about a foot away from the lead domino, and roll a marble toward it. The object is to knock down all ten dominoes with the marble. Can you do it? How many times out of ten tries will you succeed?

If you do it consistently, it's too easy for you at your age. Roll from a position farther back, or set up the dominoes so that they're spread more than ¾ inch apart. If you get really good at this, you can try various tricks, like setting the dominoes up in a curve and trying to knock them all down with one roll.

Domino Match-Ups

Divide all the dominoes evenly among all the players. If there are any dominoes left over, put them aside, out of play. Players may place their tiles on their sides so that each player can look at his own tiles, but he shouldn't show them to the other players.

Each player selects one tile and places it out on the table in front of him, facedown. On a signal, each player turns his selected tile faceup at once. The one with the highest value (combined value of all the dots on both sides of the tile) wins the other players' faceup tiles. In case of tie, nobody wins and the tiles are put aside, out of play.

Tiles that have been won are put aside in a winnings pile in front of each player, faceup. When all the tiles have been played, the player with the most tiles is declared winner. If two (or more) players have the same number of tiles, count the dots on all the tiles of the tied players, and the one with the highest value wins.

Strategy questions: Is it best to play your highest tiles first or get rid of your low tiles early? When should you play your middling tiles?

TWO
or more

MATERIALS

✐ Set of dominoes

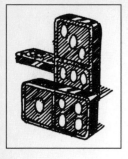

Domino Solitaire

MATERIALS

✎ Set of dominoes

Here's a neat solitaire game you can play with dominoes:

Place all the dominoes facedown, off to the side of your playing surface. Pick three and put them faceup in front of you. Choose one of the three, and put it in the middle of the playing surface. This will be the beginning of your formation. Now select another from among the unused (facedown) dominoes. Every time you play one domino on the formation, you will choose another from among the unused dominoes, just as in a regular game.

Now, if you can, play one of your three dominoes on the domino with which you started the formation. Do this in standard domino fashion by matching a six to a six, a blank to a blank, a two to a two, and so on. Play "doubles" in standard sideways domino fashion. And remember to always pick a replacement domino when you have played one.

Continue in this fashion till you've picked and played all the tiles. If you can do this, you've won. But if at any point you cannot play any of your three tiles on the formation, the game is over and you've lost.

Don't Laugh

This is a competition in which you'll try to make the other player(s) laugh without laughing yourself. While you're working at getting the other player(s) to laugh, though, he, or they, will be trying to make you laugh, too. You can tell jokes, make faces, or even make funny noises. You can remind them of funny things they've seen or silly things they've done. However, you can't touch each other. There is no tickling, poking, or any kind of touching allowed in this game.

Of course, there is this risk: As you try to make the other player(s) laugh, you may find that what you're saying or doing is so funny that you laugh at it first. Uh-oh. Now you're in trouble.

The first player to laugh loses. The last player to laugh wins.

T W O
or more

MATERIALS

✍ None

67

Dr. Dolittle

MATERIALS

✐ None; or paper, pen or pencil

Suppose you, like the famous doctor of books and movies, could talk to animals? (Well, we all talk to animals, but talk in their language . . . and understand them when they talk back.)

What questions would you ask your pet? Your friend's pet? A policeman's horse? The lion in the zoo? The monkeys? A circus elephant? Other animals?

You can simply think of the questions, or you can write them down. If you have a friend with you, she can pretend to be the various animals and answer the questions as you ask them.

Wouldn't it be fun to do this for real, though . . . and really hear what the animals have to say?

Draw a Treasure Map

It's fun to discover buried treasure . . . but it's also fun to "bury treasure" for someone else to find, then watch them search for it. Pirates buried their treasure underground; you can bury yours among the cans in the kitchen, in a corner of a closet, or . . .

What will your treasure be, and whom are you going to give the map to? Why not write a poem about your dad and hide it . . . draw a special picture for your mom . . . or hide the next test or paper on which you get a good grade? Hide surprises for friends, too.

Your map can be literally that or can be a series of instructions: "Stand in front of the living room sofa and take four baby steps toward the doorway, then turn right. Now take five giant steps forward and turn left . . ." and so forth, till you've guided them (by a deliberately confusing route) to the treasure. Or guide them by way of a riddle: "Noah's ark wasn't the only place where 'two by two' was the rule" might lead your mother to your sock drawer, where the socks are paired off in twos, and where you've hidden a pencil holder you've made for her.

O N E

MATERIALS

✐ Paper, pen or pencil

69

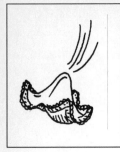

Drop the Hankie

MATERIALS

One handkerchief

Choose someone to be It. Everyone else stands in a circle, with 3 or 4 feet between each player. It stays outside the circle, holding a handkerchief (which can, of course, actually be a rag, some other piece of cloth, or a tissue). It waves the hankie, brushing the back of each player as she goes past. She chants, "I had a little dog, and he wouldn't bite you [brushing one player's back with the hankie], and he wouldn't bite you [brushing the next player's back with the hankie], and he wouldn't bite you . . ." At some point, It shouts, "But he would bite you!"

It drops the hankie to the ground behind the player she has selected and starts running around the outside of the circle. The player It has chosen quickly turns around, bends down to retrieve the hankie, stands up, and races around the circle as well. If It can get back to the empty spot where the chosen player was standing, It takes that place, and the other player becomes It. But if the other player catches It before It arrives at the safety of that spot, then It must remain as It.

When everyone's tired of it and wants to play something else, the game's over.

Dry-Land Fishing

Raining? Freezing out? Never mind—
you can go fishing anyhow . . . and
stay warm and dry! You can't eat the fish
you catch . . . but you can sure have a real
good time!

They're not real fish, you see; they're
cardboard (or, in a pinch, paper). Cut fish
shapes out of paper or cardboard, and cut
a round hole near each fish's mouth.
Color your fish with paint, crayon, or
markers, and they're ready for you to go
fishing.

Your rod and reel? A stick or ruler,
with a string tied to it, and a bent bobby
pin or hairpin tied to the other end of the
string.

Dump your fish in a broad, shallow
pan. (In a pinch, lacking a roasting pan or
dishpan or similar suitable vessel, you can
even use the bathtub.) Then try to hook
the biggest one . . . or all of them.

Don't bother weighing your catch, but
you can brag about the pretty colors of
what you caught . . . and, of course, the
one that got away!

ONE
or more

MATERIALS

✐ Large pan
(e.g., a roasting
pan or a dishpan
or something
similar), a stick
or 12-inch ruler,
string, bobby pin
or hairpin, paper
or cardboard
or tagboard,
scissors, hole
punch

✂ Optional: Crayons
or paint or
colored markers

71

MATERIALS

✐ None

Duck Duck Goose

This mildly competitive game for younger kids involves chasing and racing, no clear-cut winner, and no formal end to the game—it's over when everyone's had enough and decides to play something else.

One child is chosen to be It, and all the others crouch down in a circle. It walks around the outside of the circle, tapping each player on the shoulder and chanting "Duck" as she does. At some point of her own choosing, she instead calls, "Goose," and the player she taps on the shoulder as she calls "Goose" must now get up and chase around the circle with her. Both are trying to get back to the just-vacated space, and the first one to reach it crouches down there. The other one becomes or remains It.

Dynomatic Implosionary Elfranginating Ray Blaster

It might be made of an eggbeater and feathers. It could be constructed from a toilet paper tube with buttons glued to it. Or maybe your child's super-secret space weapon will be the result of a combination of lengths of doweling, wire coat hangers, empty candy boxes, Ping-Pong balls, or broken pieces of toys from the bottom of the toy chest or the closet shelf.

One definite ingredient is imagination; another is ingenuity.

However your child constructs it, his weapon—or maybe it will be a survey tool, or some other type of mechanism—will exercise his imagination while it brings him hours of fun for no real layout of money.

ONE
or more

MATERIALS

⬦ Whatever presents itself around the house

73

Eddie

Early Speller Safari

O N E

MATERIALS

✏ Paper, pen or pencil

Here's a game for early spellers that will help sharpen their skills. Challenge your child to find an object somewhere in the house that starts with each of the letters in his name. Depending on his spelling abilities and on the number of letters in his name, you may choose to extend the challenge to merely his first name, to his first and last name, or to his full name (if he has a middle name).

If his name is TOM, and you merely ask him to find items that begin with the letters of his first name, he might come back quickly with the following items written down: Teaspoon, Olive, Mat. Too easy? Make him find items for all the letters in THOMAS WAYNE JOHNSON. That'll keep him busy awhile!

Earth-Friendly Living

Today's kids are much more environment conscious than previous generations . . . and a good thing. Though few would disagree with the commandment to honor thy mother, we haven't been very respectful to Mother Earth.

But the same child who chided you for not recycling a can yesterday may well have carelessly tossed a candy wrapper onto the ground on his way home from school today. Kids can be as guilty as the rest of us of failing to practice what they preach.

Suggest that your child make two lists. The first? A list of the ways we all can be more Earth-friendly, from families recycling all possible items to factories reducing pollution. The second? A list of the ways your child himself can help in his own way. These might include picking up candy wrappers he sees on the street, preferring to buy paper products made from recycled materials, and bicycling wherever possible instead of asking you to drive him and send exhaust fumes into the atmosphere.

ONE
or more

MATERIALS

✐ Paper, pen or pencil

75

Edible Necklace

O N E
or more

MATERIALS

🖉 Cereal (preferably Cheerios or other doughnut-shaped cereal), Life Savers, dental floss or string, scissors

✂ Optional: Needle (for working with cereal that doesn't have holes in the middle)

An interesting necklace will result from stringing Cheerios and Life Savers on dental floss (or string). You can alternately string a piece of cereal and a piece of candy, or two Life Savers and one Cheerio, or any other arrangement that suits you.

It's not even necessary to use doughnut-shaped cereal. If you use a needle, you can string Kix, Cocoa Puffs, or other cereals. Since the design doesn't include a clasp, be sure to make the loop of dental floss large enough to slip easily over your head.

Egg-Carton Caterpillar

N o, these caterpillars won't turn into pretty butterflies, but neither will they become wool-munching moths. Make the most basic caterpillar by cutting an egg carton down the middle the long way, then turning it over, humps up, and painting it green or brown. Paint eyes on the front (up to this point, either end can be the front), add a small mouth, and you have a rudimentary caterpillar.

Instead of painting eyes on, you can use googly eyes from the crafts store. Glue two short lengths of pipe cleaner to the face for a pair of fuzzy antennae.

Now . . . you have another half an egg carton put aside . . . and your caterpillar is certainly lonely without a friend. It's an easy enough project; so . . . get busy making a companion for your first caterpillar.

O N E

MATERIALS

Egg carton, scissors, paint or crayons or markers

Optional: Pipe cleaners, googly eyes (from crafts store), glue

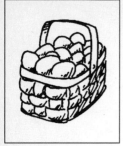

Eggshell Mosaics

MATERIALS

Black marking pen, leftover Easter eggs, glue, construction paper (colored or white) or (for greater strength) cardboard or tagboard

Easter eggs are fun to dye, fun to hide and find, pretty to look at for a little while . . . but what do you do with them after that?

Egg salad is sometimes an answer, but does your child groan when she sees the colorful shells being tossed into the garbage? Here's how she can get a second helping of enjoyment from the pretty colors:

Remove the shells from the eggs, and smash the shells into small but not tiny pieces. (You want them small enough to be pretty flat, but not so small that they're difficult to work with.) Put them aside.

Draw a picture in black marker on a sheet of construction paper or cardboard or tagboard. (The best kind of picture for this project is of one object containing several parts, such as a flower with its various petals.) Apply glue to one area of the paper, and then carefully press the eggshell pieces onto the glued area, colored side up. Work in one small area at a time, and leave the black marker outline showing.

The Eighth Dwarf?
The Tenth Planet?

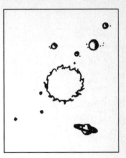

We all know the seven dwarfs' names: Sleepy, Dopey, and their friends. But what if there had been an eighth dwarf? What might he have been named?

You know the names of the nine planets, too. But what if some day science discovers a tenth planet orbiting our sun? What might they call it?

Think of names for the eighth (and ninth? tenth?) dwarf, and for any additional planets. While you're at it, what if the calendar is reorganized so the months are shorter and a thirteenth month is added; what might you call the new month? Countries often change their names. And countries are often carved up so that new countries are formed. Think of a new name for an old or new country. Suppose a new body of water is discovered—perhaps a large lake that's discovered deep in the heart of a jungle. What would you call it? If we added a new state to our country, what could we call it?

O N E
or more

MATERIALS

✎ None; or paper, pen or pencil

Family Flower . . . and Bird, and Tree

MATERIALS

None

States have official flowers, birds, and trees. Why shouldn't families? You can challenge your child to think of a suggestion for an official family flower, and so on, and to give a reason for her choice. ("I like daisies" isn't a really good reason—she's not the only member of the family. "Because of the big bed of daisies in front of the house" is a pretty good reason. "Roses should be the family flower because Mom's name is Rose" is a pretty good reason, too. So is "Buttercups should be the family flower because they're such a cheery flower and we're a cheery family.")

Now . . . how about the official bird and tree? Anything else? (Gemstones are another possibility.)

If you have more than one child, ask them to each turn in a list of suggestions.

Family Portrait Gallery

How would you like to be the family artist? Why not draw a picture of each member of the family . . . including yourself. These can be realistic likenesses or caricatures, and they can be drawn in any medium you're comfortable with, from a simple pen or pencil sketch to a full-color painted portrait.

Rather than try to copy each person's likeness exactly—unless you have great artistic skill—aim, instead, for getting a good representation of that person's most distinguishing characteristic(s). Does Dad have big bushy eyebrows? Does Mom have a cute button nose? Does your sister have a faceful of freckles? No one will question who the portrait represents when they see those eyebrows, that nose, those freckles.

ONE
or more

MATERIALS

- Paper, pen or pencil or crayons or paints or charcoals or marker

81

Family Suggestion/ Treat Box

O N E

MATERIALS

✐ Shoe box, wrapping paper or construction paper, paints or crayons, scissors, glue

First let me tell you how to make the basic box; then I'll tell you what its various uses are. Separately cover the bottom and the lid of a shoe box. You can use all-purpose (rather than Christmas or birthday) gift wrap, or you can cover it in construction paper and draw a design or pictures on the paper yourself. Glue the paper in place. Cut a slit in the lid, perhaps 5 inches long and ¼ to ½ inch wide.

Depending on the use to which the box will be put, you can label it SUGGESTION BOX or TREAT BOX or CHORE BOX or some other label. A suggestion box is one in which family members can leave suggestions for ways the family can be improved. A treat box is one in which family members can leave notes about treats they want. (These need to be affordable treats for the whole family, not just one member.) When parents decide the kids are due for a treat, they can pick a slip out of the box. Does the slip say FAMILY GOES TO THE MOVIES? or DINNER AT AN INEXPENSIVE RESTAURANT? or PIZZA DINNER? Whatever it says, that's what you're in for as a treat!

Family Timeline 1— Simple Version

There are three kinds of family timelines your child can draw (see the pages following). All three will help her get a grasp of when various events happened in relationship to others. All can be drawn on a long strip of paper, one created by taping sheets of typing paper or construction paper end to end. Then draw a long line from one end of the paper to the other. The starting date of the timeline should be at the left-hand edge of the paper so that you have room to add more years as time goes by.

The first, and simplest, kind of timeline is one that begins with your marriage and covers every year since then, with each year indicated along the timeline. Show significant highlights of family history along the timeline at the appropriate places: "Debbie born," "Ron's first communion" or "Rob's bar mitzvah," "Debbie starts school," "Rob joins Cub Scouts," and so on.

Your child can draw the timeline and fill in the events, with coaching from you.

O N E
with parental help

MATERIALS

✐ Paper, tape, fine-line marker, ruler

83

Family Timeline 2— Extended Version

Of the three kinds of family timelines your child can draw, this is the second. It works essentially the same way as the timeline just discussed, except that instead of dealing with only your immediate family, it encompasses the history of your larger family.

How far you want to go back is up to you. You can go back to the marriage of your respective parents (the kids' grandparents), or back to when your ancestors first set foot in this country, or back to any other significant point that works for you.

Divide the timeline by decades, marking off equal lengths of the line and labeling the start of each segment (e.g., 1930, 1940, 1950, and so on). At an appropriate point within each segment, mark a smaller cross line and write in the year as well as the event for each significant family happening. You'll probably want to restrict these events to births, deaths, marriages, divorces, immigration, and other truly major occurrences.

A hallway wall is a good place to hang a timeline.

Family Timeline 3— Multiple Version

The third kind of family timeline your child can draw is a variation on the first or second. Do as explained in the previous instructions, but to the significant events in family history, add significant events in national or world history that took place within the same time frame. If your timeline goes back to the 1960s, for instance, you'll want to include JFK's assassination. Which national or world history events you want to include is up to you. "Berlin Wall comes down," "Communism ends in Russia," "Challenger disaster," and "MLK's 'I Have a Dream' Speech" are certainly all good candidates for inclusion.

You might want to write the world/national events in one color of marker and the family events in a different color.

It's easier for a child to comprehend the time relationship between one event and another when she can see it depicted visually like this, whether it's two events in family history or a personal event, like the year she started school, and a national event, like the current president's election.

O N E
with parental help

MATERIALS

✐ Long strip of paper, fine-line marker

85

Find-a-Fact Safari

ONE

MATERIALS

- Encyclopedia (your own or the library's)

- Note: Your child can make this a competition with a friend working with his own encyclopedia at home

Frank Buck ("Bring 'Em Back Alive") was known for the animals he captured. And your child can be known for the facts he captures. How would he like to go to school in possession of some bit of knowledge that will really impress his friends? He can even set up a competition with one or more other friends, to see who can bring in the most fascinating fact each day.

All it takes is a tour through the encyclopedia—your own or the library's—to turn up a fascinating fact. Will he find it under Dinosaurs, under California, under Alexander Graham Bell, under Russia . . . or under some name he's never even heard of before?

Tell him he can be a bit of a show-off when he has knowledge that none of his friends has. Tell him he can be justifiably proud if he knows the names of every kind of dinosaur that has thus far been discovered.

Don't tell him this activity is educational. Let that be our little secret!

86

Fine Design

There are lots of things your child (and his friends) can design just for fun: the ideal house, a rearrangement of his bedroom, the ideal school, or even clothing. Clothing design is more likely to appeal to girls, but there's no reason boys can't design space suits, modern cowboy outfits, or new uniforms for their favorite sports teams.

As for building design or room rearrangement, there's no reason these have to be practical or realistic. If a child wants to draw a house with a brook meandering right through the middle, in which he can go fishing even in bad weather, or with a retractable sun roof for catching a tan while lying on his bed or for stargazing at night, he can certainly let his imagination run free.

The kids can cooperate on a design, working together, but it's probably better to let everyone work on his own design. This noncompetitive activity is equally good for one child or more.

ONE
or more

MATERIALS

- Paper and pencil (with eraser) for each child

87

Fingerprint Drawings

O N E
or more

MATERIALS

✏ Ink pad with washable ink, paper, pen or fine-line markers

The most fun part of this project may simply be the chance for your child to get his hands messy with permission. And the fingerprinting process is fascinating, too. If your child gets into this activity in concert with another kid, they may well divert themselves from the actual activity at hand (pun intentional!) for quite a while while they compare fingerprints and are amazed at the individual differences.

But eventually they'll tire of that and get down to the point of this activity, which is to fingerprint their hands—either thumbs only or other fingers too—and then, by dint of adding legs and tails, or arms and legs, or wings or other additions, turn those fingerprints into dogs, people, airplanes, igloos, birds, or whatever else suggests itself to them. Turn your thumbprint into a dashing young male member of royalty and you'll be justified in saying, "Someday my prints will come!"

Fishbowls

You might even see a mermaid in this fishbowl . . . if you put her there.

Start by painting a white paper plate. You can just paint a solid blue or blue-green, or you can paint waves, mermaids, starfish, rocks, old logs, or even an octopus!

You can leave the Goldfish gold, or you can paint them bright tropical colors and let them dry first; either way, glue a few to the plate. Then wrap plastic wrap around the plate.

Optional: Paint additional undersea items on the plastic wrap for a three-dimensional look.

O N E

MATERIALS

✐ Heavy white paper plates, Goldfish crackers, plastic wrap, paints and paintbrush, glue

89

Five Hundred

MATERIALS

🖎 Baseball or softball, bat, mitts

This is a batting-practice game. There's no pitcher; balls are hit fungo-style (also known as self-pitching). Decide who will bat first; the other players get out in the field. As the batter connects, the other players call the hits as they approach and keep out of each other's way as they catch the balls.

Players score by successfully fielding the ball as it's hit. When a player's score reaches 500, he becomes the new batter.

Scoring: For scooping up a ground ball, you receive 25 points; taking a ball on the second bounce, 50 points; taking a ball on the first hop, 75 points; catching a fly ball, 100 points. Negative points: For committing an error (moving to field the ball and then failing to control it cleanly), subtract the number of points the player would have earned for that particular ball had he fielded it properly.

This is not a competitive game in the usual sense: There is no one who is declared winner, and there's no formal end to the game. The game is over when the players are too tired to keep playing, or when darkness falls and they can't see the ball anymore, or when it's dinnertime.

Fizz

Related to the game of Buzz (page 29) is the game of Fizz. However, Fizz is easier to play than Buzz because multiples of 5 are easier to remember than multiples of 7. In other words, instead of saying "Buzz" for each multiple of 7 or each number that contains a 7 in it, you say "Fizz" for each multiple of 5 or each number that contains a 5 in it.

Counting in Fizz goes like this: 1 - 2 - 3 - 4 - FIZZ - 6 - 7 - 8 - 9 - FIZZ - 11 - and so on.

Otherwise the rules are the same.

TWO
or more

MATERIALS

✐ None

Fizz-Buzz

Buzz (page 29) is a fun game, and so is the previous game, Fizz. Once upon a time someone got the bright idea to combine the two; the result is a game called Fizz-Buzz.

TWO
or more

MATERIALS

✎ None

Fizz-Buzz combines both the rules of Fizz and the rules of Buzz; as a result, it's more complex. Two or more people count aloud but never say any number that contains or is a multiple of either 5 or 7.

You say "Buzz" for every number that contains a 7 or is a multiple of 7 and "Fizz" for every number that contains a 5 or is a multiple of 5: 1 - 2 - 3 - 4 - FIZZ - 6 - BUZZ - 8 - 9 - FIZZ - 11 - 12 - 13 - BUZZ - FIZZ - 16 - BUZZ - 18 - 19 - FIZZ - BUZZ - and so on. The numbers 35, 57, and 75 are either FIZZ-BUZZ or BUZZ-FIZZ—either is acceptable.

Flipping Cards

Divide a deck of cards in half, giving half to each player. You will avoid disputes ("That was my card!" "No, it was mine!") if you give one player all the red cards and the other all the black cards. Or, for a really long game, give each player a full deck, with different backs on the two decks. (For a shorter game, each player can take perhaps ten cards.)

Each player holds one card with the back up and tries to flip it in such a way that it will land faceup. Cards may not simply drop; they must turn over at least once while falling. If Player 1's card lands faceup and Player 2's card lands facedown, Player 1 collects both cards. If both cards land faceup or facedown, each player takes back his own card, and they flip again.

When one player has won all the cards, he is declared the winner. Alternative method of deciding a winner: After a set amount of time, the player with the most cards is declared the winner.

T W O

MATERIALS

✐ A deck of cards

✂ Optional: Two decks

MATERIALS

✐ Ruler, measuring tape, paper, pencil with eraser

Floor Plans

Every child needs to rearrange his room from time to time. Sometimes it's because of getting a desk (for homework). Sometimes it's because the old arrangement just doesn't work well anymore; sometimes it's simply time for a change.

The upside of a child's rearranging his room is that sometimes the new arrangement is easier to keep neat. Also, he's more likely to be inspired to work at keeping it neat for a while . . . even if the effort does wear off after a few months. The downside is that after you move the desk over there and do your best longshoreman's imitation in moving the bed to the other side of the room, he's likely to say, "I don't like it this way." Or you might even find the furniture simply doesn't fit in the new arrangement.

Ah, but he can plan it out in advance. If he draws a scale drawing of his room, complete with doors, windows, alcoves, and any other features, and then measures every piece of furniture, he can try out furniture arrangements on paper.

He can move anything and everything as many times on paper as he wants before anyone moves even a chair even an inch in real life.

Flying Shuffleboard

It's fun to prepare the materials for Flying Shuffleboard as well as to play it. Each player cuts out seven pieces of cardboard. They're strongest if cut from a carton, though standard cardboard can be used if necessary. Each player's pieces should be distinctive from those of the other player(s). One player can cut out seven stars, another all swoops, another all triangles; or each player can decorate her pieces in a distinctive color, using markers or paint.

Now lay out your target on the floor or ground. Cut differing lengths of string to form three or more circles, one within the other, in the style of a bull's-eye. The number will depend partly on how large an area you are playing in. Also, lay out a straight line of string a reasonable distance away. Players stand behind this lag line and skim their playing pieces at the target.

Give a higher value to the middle circle, increasingly lower values to the outer circles. Players score the points of the highest circle their pieces touch, even if not fully within that circle. The first player to reach 100 points (or any other number you pick) wins.

T W O

or more

MATERIALS

- Cardboard (best if cut from a sturdy carton), markers, paints and paintbrush, string, scissors

Flying Tropical Fish

MATERIALS

Newspaper, brown butcher paper or wrapping paper, stapler, paint and paintbrush, string

Your child won't have to go fishing for compliments if he has these fish hanging from his ceiling. And they're so easy, he can make them all by himself. Here's how:

Draw a large fish design on a piece of brown paper. Hold two sheets of the paper together and cut around the fish outline so that you cut two identical fish out simultaneously. Staple all around the outside of the fish, fastening the two cutouts together, but leave an opening of perhaps 5 inches through which you can later insert crumpled newspaper to stuff the fish with.

Now paint both sides of the fish— bright tropical colors are preferable, though if your son wants a silvery trout, there's no reason he shouldn't have one. Don't forget to add such details as gills, eyes, mouth, and fins.

When the paint is dry, stuff the fish and close up the 5-inch hole with staples. Find a center of balance on the back—a place where, if you hold the fish, it doesn't tip forward or backward—and staple one end of a string to that point. Staple the other end to the ceiling to hang your fish for display.

96

Football-Card Football

In this game, the 1968 Packers can play against the 1997 Dolphins . . . and possibly even win. As the old expression says, "It's all in the cards." How? It's easy.

Select two cards, one from each of two different teams (or you can pit the same team from two different years against each other, if you want). Now compare the stats of the two players whose cards you've selected. Compare everything—not just who caught the most passes but also who's taller, who weighs more, even who has the highest uniform number. Score one point for a team each time its player outscores his opponent. When you've compared all the stats, add up the points each side scored, and you've got your winner.

Two kids can play this by each selecting a card and comparing stats, but it's usually played by one kid as a competition only between two teams.

ONE
or more

MATERIALS

Paper, pen or pencil, football cards (old or new or both) or cards from other sports (if your child is more of a hockey, baseball, or basketball fan)

97

Forbidden Letters

T W O
or more

MATERIALS

✎ None

You can play this game competitively or just for fun, with as few as two players or a large group. Any player—let's say it's Danny—starts. He faces the player on his left (who we'll say is Monica), says a letter of the alphabet, and asks a question: "E. What's your favorite food?"

Monica must answer in a sentence or phrase of at least six words, answer in a way that's responsive to the question, and not use the forbidden letter in her sentence. There is no requirement for truthfulness. Monica's favorite food might in reality be egg salad; she can't say so— it has an E in it. She can't say "tomato soup"—that doesn't have an E, but it's only two words. One possible answer is, "I always chomp on radish root." Pretty silly . . . but it satisfies all the requirements.

Now Monica turns to the player on her left and states a different letter and poses a different question, perhaps "L. How do you like to spend Sundays?"

Play continues around in a circle. In a game being played strictly for fun, the game is over when the players tire of it.

Form a Rock Band . . . with Action Figures

The Army is reducing the size of its forces . . . maybe that's the reason GI Joe and his friends have left the Army and joined a rock band! (If your child is a girl, the rockers could be Barbie and her friends.)

Yes, your child's dolls and action figures can do double duty as members of a rock band. (What is your child going to name the group?) All they need are instruments—and those are easy enough to come by. An empty tuna can (or a water chestnut can, if you've recently made stir-fry, or a small cat food can, or . . .) will make a fine drum. (Parents, please check for sharp edges first.) For drumsticks, use either wooden toothpicks or headless matches. They'll also work as microphones. Cut a guitar out of cardboard. Cardboard or construction paper will also provide an amplifier.

For an extra dimension of reality, your child can turn on the stereo or radio and pretend the band is playing the songs that play.

O N E
or more

MATERIALS

✏ Action figures (e.g., GI Joe) and/or dolls of the Barbie variety, cardboard, small tin can (tuna sized), wooden toothpicks or headless matchsticks, construction paper, fine-line markers

99

ONE
or more

MATERIALS

Egg carton; twelve long, thin strips of plain white paper; scissors; pen

Fortune-Egg-ly

You've heard of fortune cookies, but have you ever heard of a fortune-telling egg carton? Pierce a slit over each of the twelve egg indentations in the carton. Each slit should be just big enough for a 1-inch piece of paper to be pushed through, but not so big that the paper will fall down inside.

Now, cut twelve long, thin strips of plain white paper. Using a pen and writing small, write a fortune on each slip. Leave a 1-inch margin with no writing at one end of the paper. The fortunes can be serious: "You will get married at age twenty-one." "You will be a great doctor." "You will live to ninety-nine." They can be funny: "You will have thirteen kids." "You will invent a new color and call it snarfle." "You will make a fool of yourself on TV."

Working from under the lid, poke each 1-inch tab through each of the twelve slits in the lid. Let the rest of the fortune rest in the cup beneath. Now close the lid. No writing should be visible on the tabs sticking up from the egg carton.

Offer the egg carton to your friends. Whichever tab of paper they pull out from the lid is their fortune.

Four-Sense Descriptions

Most of us rely more on our sense of sight than on our other senses. Yet we have four other senses as well—touch, taste, smell, and hearing. Describe as many of the items around you as you can, as well as you can, without at all mentioning how they look.

Do not taste anything not meant to be eaten or drunk. You can feel an object, shake it, or touch it to see if it makes a sound, sniff it . . . and taste it if it's appropriate. Become more aware of the other sense properties of familiar objects.

Now . . . how many familiar objects can you describe without mentioning how they look so that someone else will know what you're talking about?

O N E

MATERIALS

✐ Whatever is around you, indoors or out

Fresh, Hot Tarantulas

TWO
or more

MATERIALS

✐ A die

You're going to create a phrase, one or more adjectives followed by a noun. Player 1 starts by calling out any adjective. Player 2 then rolls the die. If a 1 comes up, roll again.

Getting to the noun involves stringing together adjectives to precede it, and each word beyond the first, which has already been called out, must begin with the letter that ended the word preceding it.

For example, if Player 1 called out BRILLIANT to start the game, then after rolling the 4, Player 2 needs to come up with an adjective beginning with T, such as TERRIFIC.

If there are more players, it is now Player 3's turn; if there are only two players, play reverts to Player 1. Let's assume Player 2 chose TASTY. Player 3 needs an adjective beginning with Y—perhaps YOUNG.

Player 4 now needs to supply a noun, since the die came up 4 and the players are now on the fourth word. It must start with a G—the letter that ended the last word. So the final phrase might be BRILLIANT, TASTY, YOUNG GIRAFFES.

There's no scoring, no winner, just laughs.

Frisbee Golf

Frisbee Golf doesn't involve clubs or balls or holes in the ground. It gets the latter part of its name because, as in actual golf, the low score wins. The standard number of holes in golf aren't requisite either . . . you can play four holes, or ten, depending on the opportunities available at your local park, on your quiet street, or in your large backyard.

You score in Frisbee Golf by hitting a previously decided-upon object with your flying disk. The "hole" can be the elm tree at the far end of your backyard, the Do Not Litter sign at the entrance of the park, the No Parking sign at the corner, the green litter basket . . . Each toss of the Frisbee counts as a stroke. The more times you have to toss the disk before you hit the object you're aiming for, the higher your score for that hole.

Like real golf, Frisbee Golf can be played in competition or by one person trying to better his previous low score.

ONE
or more

MATERIALS

- One Frisbee per player

ONE
or more

MATERIALS

✎ None; or paper, pen or pencil

"Wacky Jackie"

Funny Names

It's fun to make lists of silly or funny names. When I was a kid, we used to laugh uproariously over Etta Hamburger. Today's kids might find that less funny—they probably never heard of anyone named Etta—but they still could laugh at another of our favorites, Wanda Fonda. Other names kids might find funny include Harry Pitts, Chuck Pluck, or that perennial favorite among kids, I. P. Daly.

Try to think of as many funny names as you can. Do some of them sound particularly appropriate as names for people in some particular occupation or people with a specific hobby . . . teachers, garbage collectors, fishermen, or . . .

Geography

The player who starts off this game does so by naming any real place name—say, Michigan. The next player needs to name another place name, specifically one whose first letter is the same as the last letter of the place just named. Since Michigan ends in an N, the second player must name someplace beginning with an N: New York is a good answer. The third player—or the first player in a two-handed game—now needs a place that begins with K: Kansas. Quick—what begins with S? Sweden? Saskatchewan? South Dakota? Sonoma?

And so it goes, till one player is stumped and cannot think of a new place name beginning with the appropriate letter. (Note that the same place may not be used more than once each game—not even if there are two towns with the same name in two different states or countries, like Paris, France, and Paris, Illinois.) A player who cannot think of a new place beginning with the necessary letter is out of the game. The last player left is the winner.

T W O
or more

MATERIALS

✐ None

Ghost

MATERIALS

✐ None

✂ Optional:
Dictionary

In this spelling game, Player 1 says any letter aloud. Player 2 then adds a letter, and Player 1 now adds a letter to that. But at no point should either player complete a word with the letter he says. For instance, Player 1 says "H." Player 2 adds "E." Player 1 says "A." Player 2, thinking of HEART, says "R." But he has spelled HEAR. Uh-oh. He's completed a word.

Any time you complete a word, you get a letter toward the word GHOST. Since this is Player 2's first offense in the game, he gets a G.

Since Player 1 started the last round, Player 2 starts this round. He says "L." Player 2 says "I." He is thinking of LIGHT, which would end with Player 1. Player 1 indeed says "G," and Player 2 now says "H." Player 1 doesn't want to say "T" and get a letter, so he says "S." "I challenge you," says Player 2. Player 1 now has to name a legitimate word that begins LIGHS. But he can't think of one . . . so he gets a letter anyhow.

The first player to get all five letters, G-H-O-S-T, is out of the game.

Ghosts in the Mansion

Each player draws two grids ten boxes across by ten down. Number the across rows 1 through 10. Designate the down rows as A through J. A box is identified by the letter and number of the rows it's in. For instance, the top left box is A-1. The lowest and farthest right box is J-10.

T W O

The players sit so neither can see the other's grids. Each indicates seven ghosts on one grid by drawing a G in each box a ghost occupies. Each ghost occupies two connecting boxes, which may be side by side or above and below each other (like C-2 and C-3 or H-5 and I-5). They may not be diagonal (like D-6 and E-7).

Decide who will go first. The first player calls out a box; the opponent must truthfully answer "Ghost" or "Miss." Either way, it is now the second player's turn. Remember that even if the answer to "F-7" is "Ghost," you've only found half that ghost. Is the other half in F-6, F-8, E-7, or G-7?

Use your second grid to keep track of what squares you've called on your opponent's grid. Win by being the first player to find all the ghosts in your opponent's mansion.

Glamour Makeover

MATERIALS

- Whatever beauty supplies are around the house, a doll (if a cooperative live subject isn't available)

Clearly this is an activity for girls, and I suggest your daughter give the makeover to a willing adult "victim," rather than to a friend, so that there's someone sensible to call a halt in case things start to get out of hand. Two eight-year-olds might get into Mom's hair tint or home perm and wreak disastrous results through misuse. Even if Sara doesn't turn Eve's hair purple, Eve's mom might not love seeing her redhead come home as a brunette. But if Grandma or Mom is the makeover client, she can supervise the proceedings and still allow her daughter to have a fun time.

What will the makeover consist of? That depends both on your daughter's interest and on the "client's" willingness to be experimented with. If your daughter is at all adept with nail polish, she can give her client a manicure. A shampoo is always possible, as is something vaguely resembling a facial. How about a set— follow the shampoo up with rollers and curlers? Or the "operator" can experiment on her "client" with makeup. And let's not forget a pedicure . . . even if all that is really done is the judicious application of nail polish.

Go Surfing (on the Net)

Since not all after-school activities take place in your home or on your block, what better place is there for your child to hang out than at the library? If you don't have a computer—or if your computer lacks a modem—and you aren't wired to the Internet, suggest that your child stop at the library after school . . . for something more than just borrowing books.

O N E

Most libraries these days have computers with Internet access. And there are many child-friendly sites on the Web, many places where she can have fun and/or learn something valuable. She can do a little "virtual visiting" and get some real knowledge.

Join the library and see the world!

MATERIALS

✐ Internet access (available at your library if you don't have a computer and modem)

Grass Whistle

MATERIALS

✐ A blade of grass

This mere simple pastime won't occupy more than twenty minutes, tops, but no child should exit childhood without having learned how to turn a blade of grass into a squealing siren capable of irritating grownups in the next ZIP code.

Explain to your child that she needs to select as large and coarse a blade as possible, at least 2 inches long and preferably 3 inches or more.

To make the grass into a whistle, the child butts her thumbs together, side by side. The grass is held in place at its ends by the base of the thumb and the bulge of the thumb joint. The edge of the grass blade will be visible in the open space between the two joints.

The child holds the backs of her thumbs against her lips and blows through the space between them. The grass blade will begin to vibrate at a high rate, and a piercing shriek or whistle is the result.

Very little practice is required before a child is an expert at producing skull-splitting sounds from an innocent blade of grass. Always prepare for this activity by having on hand enormous quantities of the child's favorite snack treats, with which you can try to bribe her to quit making that noise.

The Great Detective

This is a test of your powers of observation. How much do you notice of the world around you? It's not a test that you pass or fail, and it's not a competitive activity, though two or more can play.

The test isn't timed. Take as long as you want. The idea is to describe a person or place, not including the room you're currently in or a person who's in the room with you. Write down as many visual details as you can think of about that place or that person. Then, when you've written down everything you can think of, check your powers of observation by taking your list with you while you look at the person or place you've described.

If you've described a room in your house or a person who's currently in the house, you can check yourself right then. If not, check it out at the earliest possible opportunity. Go into the schoolroom, the room in your best friend's house, or wherever, or visit the person you've described. How many details did you get right? How many did you get wrong? How many things did you simply not write down at all?

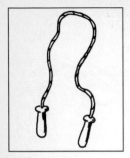

Grounded Jump-Rope Game 1

O N E
or more

MATERIALS

✐ Long jump rope
or length of
clothesline

This jump-rope game doesn't involve any jumping in the traditional manner. The jump rope remains firmly on the ground at all times. As with traditional jump-rope games, the participant can play by herself or with others, either in competition or in a cooperative spirit of "Let's see if we can all do it."

A long length of rope (such as might be used when two "turners" are turning the rope for a third player to jump) is needed here, rather than the shorter length a solo player would ordinarily jump with. You don't need a commercial jump rope; clothesline or any other kind of rope is fine. But you do want something thicker than a piece of string so that a player knows for sure if she has stepped on the rope.

Stretch the rope out as tight and straight as you can, but don't anchor the ends; if you do get your feet tangled in the rope, you don't want to be caught and tripped. Jump with both feet from one side of the rope to the other as you move forward. Each move must take you both forward and to the other side of the rope simultaneously. Do it without stepping on, tripping over, or touching the rope.

Grounded Jump-Rope Game 2

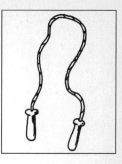

L ike the game that preceded it, this jump-rope game doesn't involve jumping in the traditional manner, as the jump rope remains firmly on the ground at all times. Again, this is a game your child can play alone or in competition with others. Again, too, a long length of rope is what's needed. And again, you need to stretch the rope out as tight and straight as you can, without anchoring the ends, for safety's sake.

Standing to the left of one end of the rope, put your right foot down alongside the rope. Now take a baby step forward and put your left foot down to the right of the rope. Take another baby step forward, putting your right foot down to the left of the rope again. Continue walking in this manner, trying to walk quickly, till you reach the end of the rope. Can you do it without tripping and without stepping on or touching the rope?

O N E
or more

MATERIALS

✐ Long jump rope or length of clothesline

113

"Grow" an Indoor Garden

** O N E**

MATERIALS

Green pipe cleaner, colored construction paper, scissors, crayons, glue, clay, flowerpot

How does your garden grow? Many kids' gardens "grow" indoors . . . needing no green thumb, just a carefully wielded scissors.

A green pipe cleaner forms each flower's stem, with blossoms cut from construction paper. These flower need not look like real tulips or daisies. Since your child is creating them, why shouldn't she design them too? She can cut out blossoms that resemble real flowers, or she can fashion red daisies, purple roses, or flowers whose shapes look nothing like any real-life greenery.

Cut the blossoms from construction paper, using crayons to color the centers a different hue, or to give the flower alternating-colored petals. Then attach the blossom to the green pipe cleaner. (Either use glue or make a crimp or z-bend just below the top of the pipe cleaner, then stick the pipe cleaner through the center of the blossom. The crimp or z-bend will hold the blossom in place so that it doesn't slide down the stem.)

"Plant" the flower in a flowerpot by sticking the bottom end of the stem into a flattened ball of clay, then inserting the clay in a flowerpot.

"Grow" New Crayons

Why throw away old crayons? They can be recycled to create new ones . . . in "mystery shades." Here's how:

Preheat the oven to 200°. Separate your crayon stubs into color families—blues and purples, greens, reds and pinks, yellows and oranges, neutrals. For each color family for which you have crayon stubs, you want to create one form to melt them in. Do this by wrapping a double layer of aluminum foil slightly more than halfway around a whole crayon, then removing the crayon.

Now remove the paper from your crayon stubs and put all the stubs from each color family into one form. Make sure that the ends are turned up so that when the crayon stubs melt, they don't ooze out of the forms. Line a cookie sheet with aluminum foil and put the forms onto the lined cookie sheet. Place the whole thing in the oven for around ten minutes, then remove and allow to cool for around half an hour. The resultant crayons won't be perfectly rounded and smooth but will be very intriguing colors.

O N E
with parental help
as appropriate in
use of oven

MATERIALS

Stubs of old crayons, cookie sheet, aluminum foil, pot holders, whole crayon

Guess the Number

or more (and the more, the better), with parental help nearby to settle disputes

MATERIALS

Paper, pens or pencils

Each player thinks of three questions to which the answer is a number. Here are some examples: How many baseball players are on the field at one time? How many sides does a pentagon have? How many pennies do two dimes and four nickels equal? How many inches are in a yard? One at a time, each player asks his questions aloud.

If there are only two players, the opponent can answer the questions aloud; if there are three or more players, each player should write down his answers. Score a point for each correct answer. When each player's questions have been asked and answered, add up the score. The highest score wins.

Gumdrop Drop

Play this game on a sidewalk or in the street of a traffic-safe cul de sac. With chalk, draw ten or twelve circles roughly three times the size of a gumdrop. These circles should themselves form a circle. Leave at least the width of one gumdrop between each circle.

Mark with chalk a point value in each circle. These point values shouldn't increase or decrease steadily around the circle, but rather be at random, such as 2, 7, 5, 9, 3, 1, 11, 6, 12, 4.

Draw a lag line about half a foot away from the nearest part of the big circle. Players stand behind that line, reach forward, and try to drop the gumdrop so that it lands at least partly within one of the circles. If it does, that player earns the point value of that circle. If it lands fully within a circle, it earns double the point value of that circle.

Each player drops the gumdrop one at a time. Play proceeds from the first player to the second, and then to any other players one at a time, then back to the first player again.

The game ends when each player has had ten turns. The player with the highest score wins.

TWO
or more

MATERIALS

✐ Chalk, gumdrops

117

Handprint Tulips

MATERIALS

Finger paints in red, yellow, and purple; bowls; regular paint in green; paintbrush; paper; newspaper to work over

This one's not only easy, it's messy . . . and kids just love messy fun! But spread out newspapers, and you should emerge from the fun with your house undamaged!

Here's how your child goes about making handprint tulips:

Put red, yellow, and purple finger paints in bowls. Dip your hand in each color, one at a time, and press your hand down on a piece of paper, with your fingers and thumb held together, not spread out. You can make one or more of each color of handprint. Wash your hands between each color, and again when you're done making handprints.

Now, with regular paint, paint a thickish green line downward from each handprint. The handprints are your tulips, and the green lines are their stems. You can add green blades of grass if you want, though that isn't at all necessary.

Such pretty tulips . . . and you can truly say they're "handmade"!

Hang a Motto or Banner

Got a favorite saying? Got something you really believe in? Hang those words on your wall for all the world to see! It might be a quote from your favorite book or movie, a motto or proverb you believe in, or something you've said so often that your friends automatically connect those words with you.

O N E

MATERIALS

✏ Marking pen or computer, paper, paints or colored markers

✂ Optional: Scissors

If you've got a computer, you can type the words in, then print them out in large fancy letters. Or you can choose to just print them on paper, using large block letters.

You can decorate the sheet of paper with pictures of flowers, animals, geometric designs (triangles, squares, circles, rectangles), or curlicues. You can cut the paper into a triangle (pennant shape), or give it scalloped edges, or cut it in some other attractive way.

Why not make several motto banners and give them as gifts to your friends, grandparents, or favorite teacher?

I have this motto on my wall: DON'T WAIT FOR YOUR SHIP TO COME IN . . . SWIM OUT TO IT. What's yours going to say?

119

Hanging Jack-o'-lantern

ONE

MATERIALS

✎ Wire hanger
(check for sharp,
pointed, exposed
ends), nylon
stocking,
construction
paper, glue

This is a project for an older child—
working with wire hangers is not a
suitable project for a five-year-old, nor is
this project within that age's capability.
The first step in this activity is to try to
bend a wire hanger into as close to a good
circle as possible, which isn't terribly easy.
(Don't bend the hook of the hanger; that
remains as is.)

Once that's been accomplished, the
rest is easy. The child pulls an old nylon
stocking over the hanger, tying a knot at
the top, but below the hanger's hook.
Then he ties another knot at the bottom,
making the nylon taut. From construction
paper, he cuts a proper jack-o'-lantern
nose, mouth, and eyes, which he glues
onto the nylon.

The jack-o'-lantern can be hung by the
hanger's hook on a doorknob, cabinet
knob, nail, or picture hook.

Happy Judy Day!

There really already is a day—our birthday—that celebrates each of us every year. But in the midst of all the excitement over parties and presents, most of us don't celebrate the birthday person any other way, or if we do, such celebration is minimal. And adults tend to get left out of being the recipients of birthday foofawraw altogether in most households. There are Mother's Day and Father's Day, but those days celebrate all mothers or fathers.

What if each family member—regardless of age—got to pick a day—any calendar day that didn't already belong to another family member—and claim it as his or her own?

How would your child like to have her day celebrated? Ask her to make a list of suitable forms of celebration. Would she choose to sleep late? Be served breakfast in bed or in the yard? Go out to eat breakfast in a restaurant? And the rest of the day . . .

You could also ask her to think of ways to celebrate other family members' special days as well, especially yours.

O N E

MATERIALS

✐ None; or paper, pen or pencil

121

Heart-Themed Wrapping Paper

MATERIALS

Scissors; large sheets of paper (preferably white); glue; hearts of varied sizes that your child has cut out of magazine pictures (or ads), old recycled gift wrap, color comic strips, or anywhere else she can find them (greeting cards are not a suitable source because the paper is too thick and stiff)

Hearts are suitable for gift wrap for almost any occasion—not just Valentine's Day, but any holiday when love is a suitable expression, such as birthdays, Mother's Day, or Father's Day.

Your child will need to cut hearts out of anywhere she can find them (as explained under "Materials"). If she plans ahead, she can collect these hearts for a while and have them on hand when she's ready to undertake this project. She should trim tightly as she cuts the hearts out so that none of the background shows.

Then all she needs to do is glue them onto plain, preferably white paper. She can glue them collage-style, with one heart overlapping another, or she can space them out. Either way, she now has a sheet of wrapping paper—or several, depending on the number of hearts she was able to find—with which she can wrap future presents most distinctively . . . and lovingly.

Hey—I'm Oprah!

Your child on TV? Well, not really . . . but she can pretend. Maybe she has a future as a talk show host; maybe not, but it's still fun to pretend she's Oprah (or Jerry or Sally Jessy—or even that she's herself, all grown up and starring on TV) and hosting a show.

TWO
or more

MATERIALS

✎ None

Her friend(s) or sibling(s) can be her guest(s), either playing themselves or taking the part of interesting guests on Oprah's show. The subjects discussed can be typical talk show fare or celebrity chatter, or they can be the topics dear to every kid's heart: "Do you think teachers give too much homework?" "Should schools require every child to wear a uniform?" "Should PE be a mandatory class?" "Is there much cheating going on during tests in schools these days?"

123

Hippopotamus

TWO
or more

MATERIALS

✎ None

Here's another game (see Beep!) that requires players to avoid saying certain letters. For this game, players really have to be pretty good spellers—this isn't a game for the average seven-year-old, though a pair or group of ten-year-olds can have a hysterically good time with it.

Player 1 chooses a key word and says it aloud—perhaps CIRCUS. Player 2 now has to say the alphabet aloud pretty quickly. But any time he comes to any of the letters in the key word CIRCUS, he must instead say "Hippopotamus": A - B - Hippopotamus - D - E - F - G - H - Hippopotamus - J - K - L - M - N - O - P - Q - Hippopotamus - Hippopotamus - T - Hippopotamus - V - W - X - Y - Z.

Obviously it's no fun—too easy—if you choose a really short key word, such as TOE or EAT. And it's too complicated and really unfair to choose a terrifically long word. The game may be played competitively, in which case a player who messes up is out of the game, or it may be played strictly for laughs.

124

Holiday Braid

Your child surely knows how to braid—from making lariats in Arts and Crafts, perhaps from braiding her hair. But has she ever thought of braiding yarn to make a holiday-themed decoration for her room?

All she has to do is neatly braid several long lengths of yarn, colored appropriately to the holiday in question, and drape them across the top of her room doorway, her closet doorway, her headboard, or in any other suitable place. They give a festive air to any room in the house.

O N E

MATERIALS

- Yarn in colors suitable for any holiday or season (e.g., orange, brown, and black for Halloween; red, white, and blue for patriotic holidays; red and green and perhaps snow-white for Christmas; red, white, and pink for Valentine's Day; fall colors for autumn; pastels for spring)

Homemade Double Jigsaw Puzzle

O N E

MATERIALS

Piece of cardboard (8½-by-11-inch or similar size), two pictures cut from magazines that are the same size as the cardboard, scissors, glue

Though it will be fun to hand this jigsaw puzzle to a friend later on and say, "Put this together if you can," creating the puzzle is a solo endeavor. You'll need two magazine pictures (they can come from ads) that are close to each other in size. You don't want a large picture of a person; the ideal pictures will show many smaller things—perhaps a busy street with several stores on it, or a woods with many trees, or a large body of water—and both pictures should look somewhat similar to each other. That is, you don't want a predominantly green forest scene and a predominantly blue lake scene.

If the pictures aren't quite 8½ by 11 inches in size, you can certainly choose a picture that's, say, 9 by 10 inches and cut down another picture so that it, too, is 9 by 10 inches.

Glue both pictures to the cardboard, one on each side. Give the glue a chance to dry. Then cut the cardboard into odd-shaped pieces, in jigsaw puzzle fashion. Mix the pieces up.

Now try to put the puzzle back together . . . or give it to a friend and let him try.

Homemade Greeting Cards

Your child can make homemade greeting cards for family and friends' birthdays, other occasions, keep-in-touch, and even for sale to other kids in a modern-day version of the lemonade stand.

For younger kids, all that's needed is to cut and fold either typing paper or construction paper, then draw a picture on the front and add a greeting, such as HAPPY BIRTHDAY or HAPPY HALLOWEEN or MERRY CHRISTMAS. On the inside, add a few more appropriate words.

Older kids, of course, can emulate commercial greeting cards more closely, with a greeting that begins on the outside and continues on the inside. It can be humorous, with a punch line when you open the card, or sweet, with complimentary words inside.

O N E

MATERIALS

✐ Construction paper or typing paper, colored fine-line markers, scissors

✄ Optional: Glitter and glue

127

Homemade Jigsaw Puzzles

MATERIALS

- Magazine, cardboard or tagboard, glue or paste, pencil, scissors
- Optional: Crayons

Your child can create his own jigsaw puzzles by cutting out interesting and colorful pictures from magazines and pasting them down on cardboard or tagboard (or even old filing folders). The pictures can be magazine illustrations or even parts of ads. As an alternative, he can also draw his own picture directly on the cardboard.

After a picture is pasted or drawn on the cardboard, the child takes a pencil and draws the design for the cut lines on the back of his cardboard. To minimize frustration, the number of cuts should be kept small. Even so, parental help may be needed with the cutting.

Here's where having more than one player becomes more fun: After each child has cut up her own picture (or had a parent help), it's great fun to trade pictures. Each child now has to put together the puzzle the other child cut up.

Horse

Choose the order in which the players will shoot at the basket. The player who shoots first is the leader; the others must copy both the type of shot he makes and the place from which he shoots. If the leader fails to make his shot, he isn't penalized, but he loses his position as leader, and the next player in line becomes leader. If, however, the leader does make the shot, everyone else has one chance to try to make the shot. Any subsequent player who fails to do so acquires an H (as in HORSE, the name of the game).

T W O
or more

MATERIALS

Basketball and hoop

Now the next round starts, with the next player in turn becoming the leader, and with the leader making a different shot from a different place. All the same rules apply, except that a player who already has an H and misses a shot now gets an O. (And the next time he would get an R, and so on.)

The leader is always free to choose whatever type of shot he wants, from whatever location he wishes, including both basic shots and trick shots. A player who has all five letters of the word HORSE is out of the game. The last person left is the winner.

House Number Math

MATERIALS

Paper, pencil

Here's some fun for the math-minded child. Take your house number and play around with it. Assuming you don't have a single-digit number (3 Cherokee Lane, for instance), take your house number and reverse it. (If you live at 57 Mockingbird Court, reversing it would give you 75.) Subtract the smaller number from the larger one. What do you get? (In this case, you'd get 18.) Add the digits together, and what do you get? (In this case, 9.) By any chance, does that equal your child's age?

Other "experiments": Subtract child's age from house number. Add digits of result together. Add ages of all the kids in the family and then add the digits of the result together. Add the digits of your house number together, then add in the number of people in the family. Add your phone number to your house number and then add up the digits. Or add all the digits of the two numbers first (different result). How many of these experiments will result in the child's age? ("It adds up to me!") How many will result in other seemingly significant numbers?

Household Scavenger Hunt

You, the parent, need to help with this one. How difficult you make the hunt's qualifications will depend on the age of your child. Basically what you're asking him to do is to find either as many different objects as he can that fit a certain qualification, or else one in each room of the house. (For instance, you might ask him to find striped things or green things or oval things or metal things, or any other qualification you can think of.)

He's not to literally bring you everything he finds. Rather, you'll ask him to write down the things he found (e.g., "candy dish on coffee table" or "egg timer in kitchen"). You'll perhaps need to set some rules (e.g., "No opening drawers" or "No going into Dad's tool kit").

You can challenge him to find one item of that qualification in every room of the house, or you can say, "You have twenty minutes to see how many plaid things you can find in the house—not counting clothes."

O N E
with parental help

MATERIALS

✐ Paper, pen or pencil

131

MATERIALS

One or more
lengths of rope
(preferably cotton
clothesline rope),
a manual on tying
knots (the Boy
Scout Manual is
great for this)

How Knot to Be Bored

Trial and error is lots of fun when you're learning to tie knots . . . and really there are no "errors"—at least none that can cause any real harm, so long as the child is old enough to know not to involve the family dog in the project! At worst, a knot won't hold or, perhaps, will be difficult to get unknotted. Neither of these qualifies as one of Life's Major Problems.

After fooling around on her own for a while with the rope, your child may want to consult a good authority on tying knots—the Boy Scout Manual is one of the most recommended. From such an authority, she can learn the proper way to tie more knots that she could possibly figure out on her own.

I "Can" Score— Indoors

There are various games your child can play with a Ping-Pong ball, one or more coffee cans, and a newspaper club. To make the newspaper club, roll a section (or two thin ones) of newspaper up tightly and secure it closed with masking tape or package sealing tape or other heavy tape. (Instead of a newspaper club, your child can use a yardstick.)

A simple game involves merely aiming the ball at the can from a distance. (Parental caution: Examine the coffee cans yourself to be sure they're free of sharp edges.) If the player can get the ball into the can from, say, 4 feet away, she scores, even if the ball bounces out again. She can try this ten times and see how many goals she scores out of ten tries. Then she can try it another ten times to see if she improves her average. Or she can play competitively against another child.

Variations: You can remove both ends of the can and require that the ball go clear through the can in order to score. Or the player can try trick shots, such as standing with her back to the can and hitting the ball between her legs.

ONE
or more

MATERIALS

✐ Newspaper, heavy tape, Ping-Pong ball, empty coffee can(s)

✂ Optional: A yardstick

133

I "Can" Score— Outdoors

O N E
or more

MATERIALS

✐ Newspaper, heavy tape, Ping-Pong ball, empty coffee can(s)

✂ Optional: A yardstick

The same newspaper club, Ping-Pong ball, and coffee cans that worked for the activities on the preceding page will also come in handy outdoors. (Parental caution: Examine the coffee cans yourself to be sure they're free of sharp edges.) Again, a yardstick can be substituted for the newspaper club.

Your child can set up cans in various locations all around the yard, turning it into a miniature golf course. (If your yard isn't large enough for a nine-hole course, there's no reason this can't be a four-hole course, or a seven-hole course.)

Variation: She can set up three cans in a row, with some space between them, all three cans having had both ends removed, and try to hit the ball through all three of them.

"I Have a Large Nose"

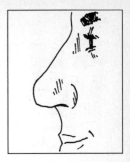

Player 1, leading off this game, says, "I have a large nose," and points to any other part of her anatomy . . . let's say it's her knee. Player 2 repeats the statement, "I have a large nose," echoing the gesture as well and pointing to her knee. Then she adds further description. She might say, "and long hair," and she might point to her big toe. Now Player 3—or Player 1 again, in a two-player game—repeats what has been said and done before and adds something to it: "I have a large nose [points to knee] and long hair [points to big toe] and green teeth [points to ear]."

Players must continue in this way. Any player who repeats a wrong body part or points to a wrong one—or who actually points to the part of the body that has just been mentioned—is out of the game. The last one left in the game is the winner.

TWO
or more

MATERIALS

✐ None

"I Make a Motion"

THREE
or more

MATERIALS

✐ None

This game is played standing in a circle. Choose one person to start. That person says, "I make a motion that we . . ." and then adds an actual motion, like "stamp our feet," which she does as she says it. The next player clockwise in the circle again says, "I make a motion that we . . ." and adds a different motion, perhaps "nod our heads." He then nods his head, after which he stamps his feet. The next player goes through the same rigmarole, naming a motion and doing it, then repeating the other two players' motions in order.

Play continues in this manner, from player to player around the circle, with each player adding a motion, verbally and physically, and repeating the other players' motions in order physically. Any player who leaves out a motion, does the motions in the wrong order, or in any other way messes up, is out of the game. The last player left is the winner.

"I Want to Sell You a Kangaroo"

Your child will need all his glibness as he pretends to be a salesman with a most unusual item to sell. It's his job to persuade his "customer" that indeed she wants to buy the item in question . . . which might be the kangaroo of this game's title, or a spiderweb, or a wooden horse from an old merry-go-round, or . . .

The customer starts the game, saying, "How much do you want for that kangaroo?" It's then up to the salesman to name a price and continue by extolling the virtues and uses of the item in question.

The customer is free to answer, "I'll take one," or "Not today, thank you," or otherwise, but then the salesman turns around and becomes the customer, asking, "And what do you want for that spiderweb?" or some other item. The former customer, now salesman, might suggest he buy a spiderweb so he can decorate his house with it for Halloween, as a bed for his pet spider, or to keep his younger, spider-fearing sister out of his room. (As you can see, the uses can range from fanciful to nearly realistic.) There's no winner or loser in this game, and no formal end.

T W O

MATERIALS

✐ None

137

I.D. Game

T W O
or more

MATERIALS

✐ Empty bag, familiar objects

How well can you recognize familiar objects by just the way they feel? Here's a game your child can play with one or more friends, siblings, and even parents:

Take a familiar object and put it in an empty bag. Have another person feel the object without looking into the bag. See if she can guess what it is. Then let her do the same with you.

There is no time limit. You are not competing against each other, only against yourself. If you guess right, you're a winner. There can be two or more winners—in fact, if everyone who's playing guesses right, then everyone is a winner.

If I Ruled the Island . . .

ONE
or more

MATERIALS

Paper, pen or pencil

Here's the proposition behind this activity: Your child is an explorer, and in sailing the seas, she's just come upon a whole undiscovered island! There are people on this island, but there's no form of government, and things are a tad . . . well, disorganized and undisciplined. What to do?

Your child is there . . . surely she can fix things up so the inhabitants have a proper government, one that can rule the island nation successfully and restore order to the chaos. But what would she recommend? What form of government? What sort of organization? What rules and principles and values should govern the day-to-day lives of these inhabitants?

Frankly, this is an activity that at once both delights kids—what kid doesn't relish the chance to be The Boss, if only in her imagination?—and at the same time teaches them this lesson: that rules are necessary, that anarchy is undesirable, that there has to be some sort of restraint in place.

If Queen Isabella Met President Kennedy . . .

O N E
or more

MATERIALS

✎ None; or paper, pen or pencil

Suppose Queen Isabella had met President Kennedy. Do you imagine they'd have a lot to say to each other about running a country? Or maybe Queen Isabella would be more interested in what America turned out to be like, so many years after Columbus discovered it, and President Kennedy would be more interested in learning what people's hopes were for the future of the new land when it was discovered.

Imagine that any two people from history—or one person from history and one who's alive today—met each other. Just what would they talk about? You can speak the conversation aloud, taking each person's part in turn, or you can write it down on paper.

If you have a friend with you, you can take one person's part . . . say, Pocohontas. And she can be the other person . . . say, Betsy Ross.

You can also do this with fictional characters. Suppose Snow White met the Big Bad Wolf! Invent a conversation between them.

140

Illustrate a Story

Sometimes the pictures in a book are almost as good as the story. But do you sometimes think, "That's not what I think he looks like"? Or are you now reading chapter books with fewer illustrations, and illustrations that perhaps are all in black and white?

Why not draw your own illustrations for your favorite book? Please understand—I'm not suggesting you draw in the book. But you can draw pictures on separate sheets of paper and tuck them into the appropriate places in the book, whether it's a picture book or a chapter book.

Now you can illustrate your favorite books the way you want to see the characters pictured.

O N E

MATERIALS

⬨ Paper, crayons or paints or colored markers

"I'm Going Shopping"

TWO
or more

MATERIALS

✐ None

In this variation on the remember-a-list theme, the players have a little help for their memories: The first player's item must begin with A, the second player's with B, the third with C, and so forth. The items can be grocery products but don't need to be. Each player has to repeat what was said by the previous players. Here's an example of a three-player game:

Player 1: "I'm going shopping, and I'm buying apples." Player 2: "I'm going shopping, and I'm buying apples and bananas." Player 3: "I'm going shopping, and I'm buying apples, bananas, and candy." Player 1: "I'm going shopping, and I'm buying apples, bananas, candy, and dogs." Player 2: "I'm going shopping, and I'm buying apples, bananas, candy, dogs, and Easter eggs."

Play continues in this way until a player messes up, either by getting items out of order, by failing to remember an item correctly, or by being unable to supply an item for her letter. (The more difficult letters shouldn't provide a problem—shoppers can by xylophones, queens, and zebras, though it's rare that the game ever gets that far.)

The Improv Game

This game bears a good bit of similarity to Pick-a-Plot (page 237), but instead of writing a story, in this game your child is asked to act the story out.

The instructions here are for two participants. If more kids are playing, several can participate at once, or two can act at a time while the others sit and watch, waiting their turns.

Prepare by putting ten or even twenty folded slips of paper into each bowl. In one bowl, you'll put descriptions of people (e.g., a spaceman, a zookeeper, a burglar, a Girl Scout, a principal, a deaf person, a pet shop owner). In the second bowl, you'll put descriptions of places (e.g., in school, in the supermarket, in a cave, on Mars, at an amusement park, in a TV studio). And in the last bowl, you'll put descriptions of situations (e.g., gets a bad toothache, has a flat tire, can't find someone, can't stop laughing, wins the lottery, inherits a comic book factory, finds a mysterious map).

Each of the two players draws one slip of paper identifying the character each will play. One or the other of them draws a slip telling where the action will take place and, then, what the situation will be. Then they improvise a scene.

TWO
or more

MATERIALS

✐ Three bowls or hats or other containers, paper, pen or pencil, scissors

143

The Incredible Adventures of Jon Green

O N E

MATERIALS

⬦ None; or paper, pen or pencil

Write a story about yourself. Not a true story . . . but a totally untrue piece of fiction. Substitute your name for the name Jon Green and you'll get the idea of what this activity is about. Now, it's not nice to lie. You should never make up stories about yourself and pass them off as true. But writing fiction is a totally different matter.

As long as you tell people it's just a story, you can write about how you went undersea in a submarine, going so deep that you were able to pass right under North America and come out on the other side. What fabulous creatures did you see when your submarine shone its headlight under the murky waters? Did you discover a tribe of mermaids? An underwater oil well? A new supply of gold? A totally new kind of seaweed that when boiled into a tea cures every illness people can possibly get?

If you like your story, why not write it down so you don't forget it? And then think up another one.

Initials

Here's a game that no one named Zoe will want to play . . . or Quentin, or anyone last-named Quillen or Zuckerman, either. As you may have guessed, initials play a large part in the game.

One player, the first Questioner, asks the other player a question. The reply doesn't have to be honest, but it must be composed of two words that begin with the player's initials and are responsive to the question. For example, if the Questioner asks, "What did you do today?" I might answer, "Crush mangoes," since my name is Cynthia MacGregor. To "What's your favorite food?" I might reply, "Charred muskrat." To "Where did you go on your vacation?" I might say, "Crossed Mississippi."

After the Questioner asks one question of the other player, that player becomes the Questioner and asks a question of the first player.

This game can be played competitively or just for fun. In the competitive version, each player has five seconds (ten for younger kids) to come up with a reply. He's out if he fails to reply within that time, replies with an answer that doesn't begin with the right letters, or uses an answer that's already been used.

MATERIALS

✐ None

Initials . . . Title . . . Story

Here's another game whose rules are simple but demanding: Player 1 names from three to five letters (excluding Q, Z, X, U, and Y), and Player 2 has to think of a title for a story or book, the words in which begin with those letters . . . in any order. He may not add any other words, except for A, AN, AND, and THE.

Player 1 then has to briefly tell a story, or tell the synopsis of a book, that is suggested to her by that title. For example, if Player 1 says, "G, L, T, and N," Player 2 might respond, "A Great Night to Laugh," or "Let's Go to Nebraska," or "Teresa Needs Large Glasses," or "Ted Gets Noisy Laughing." And Player 1 then has to make up a story based on that title.

Then trade places. Player 2 thinks up the initials, Player 1 decides on a title that starts with those initials, and Player 2 is required to write the story.

Again, there's no winner or loser, just lots of fun.

Invent a Food

ONE
with parental help
as appropriate in
use of oven

MATERIALS

Pen, paper,
whatever food is
handy in the
kitchen

Some foods are pretty straightforward:
a plain fried pork chop, a turkey
sandwich on rye bread with mayo. Other
foods, though, can get unbelievably
creative, especially some sandwich
combinations.

Suppose that instead of just putting
that turkey on rye with mayo, you built the
sandwich on an English muffin instead of
rye bread and used Russian dressing
instead of mayo? Suppose you added
some other stuff to the turkey . . . maybe
some strips of bacon, a slice of tomato,
some cole slaw, some ham, and some
sliced water chestnuts? Do you think that
would be good?

What if you seasoned the fried pork
chop with garlic? Or cooked it in cream of
mushroom soup after browning it, instead
of just frying it? Or covered it with fried
onions and mushrooms?

Think about foods you like—which two
(or more) of them would go well together?
Maybe salami and melted cheese? What
goes with peanut butter besides jelly?
Invent a recipe and write it down.

If your child is old enough, consider
letting him actually try to prepare the food
he's dreamed up—perhaps with help from
you as needed.

Invent a Game

O N E
or more

MATERIALS

✐ Varied

If you draw a circle on the pavement with chalk and then try to throw a rock at the circle, that's a pastime. To make the activity even more fun, add some specifics, some rules to the activity: You have to stand back of the maple tree when you're throwing. You get three tries. If you get the rock inside the circle once during the three tries, you've won, and if you get it inside the circle all three times, you get a bonus point.

You've now invented a game.

Every game has rules and an objective. A game can be for one player, for two, or for several. It can be an active game like tag or a quiet game like most word games. It can be played indoors or outdoors or either. It can require a game board or other special equipment (like a deck of cards), just a pencil and paper, or nothing at all. It can be totally unique or a variation on an existing game.

The next time your child is at loose ends with nothing she feels like doing, why not suggest she invent a new game? (See also Create a Board Game, page 54.)

148

Invent a Holiday—
Version 1

What the world needs is . . . more holidays! Your child just decreed it, and since she's also declared herself queen of the world, that makes it so.

Or so she wishes! Well, she can't really declare a no-school day in the middle of May, but she can dream, can't she? This activity takes two forms, the imaginative and the practical. This is the imaginative version; the practical version follows.

For the imaginative version of inventing a holiday, your child will decide when the new holiday is to be celebrated (perhaps in a month when there aren't many days off school), what it celebrates, and how the world (or the country) should celebrate it. Should there be special food? Fireworks? Or is it a more solemn occasion? Would people dress a special way? What else would mark the occasion?

The president isn't likely to ever take her up on her idea and make it official, but we all know it's fun to dream.

O N E
or more

MATERIALS

✐ None

September 12th "Happy Cole Family Day!"

O N E
or more

MATERIALS

✐ None

Invent a Holiday— Version 2

Your family can have a special holiday all its own. Of course it won't be a day off school for your child (or off work for you), but there are plenty of other ways you can celebrate it.

First your child needs to decide what the holiday celebrates. The day the first of your ancestors arrived in this country? The first day of spring, because your family particularly enjoys outdoors activities? Kindness Day, Happiness Day, or Charitable Day? Or simply [Your Family Name] Day?

Now decide on a fitting date for celebrating the holiday. And last, decide on the way it should be celebrated. Remember that this is for real. It's not just wishful thinking, as in the preceding activity. So her suggestions have to be practical. Will you celebrate it by going on a picnic? Having a family field day with races and water balloon fights in the park or backyard? Honoring your ancestors? Looking through old photo albums? Is there a particular food that's going to become traditional for celebrating Courage Day or the Johnson Family Summer Solstice Celebration?

Invent a New Dance

Where do new dances come from? Every dance was invented by someone—or some group of people. From the fox trot to the frug, from disco dancing to the tango, from the lindy hop to the bunny hop, the macarena to the mashed potatoes, every dance craze over the years and every enduring dance that is still performed to the beat of music was invented by somebody.

ONE
or more

MATERIALS

✐ None

Why not your child?

Suggest that he let his feet move to the music and see what he comes up with. He can approach it methodically, analyzing the steps of other dances and thinking about what makes for a good set of steps, or he can just put on some music and let the sounds and the beat inspire his feet.

If he's got friends over, they can even work on this as a cooperative project.

Invisible Ink Messages

O N E
or more

MATERIALS

Lemon, bowl,
paper, toothpick

You don't have to send away to a firm that's advertising in the back of a comic book in order to get your hands on some invisible ink. You probably have invisible ink in your fridge right now . . . and if not, it's as close as your supermarket. I'm talking about lemon juice.

Squeeze a lemon into a bowl, dip a toothpick into the juice, and start writing. The faint letters that cross the page will disappear as they dry.

But never fear . . . if the recipient of the missive knows the secret, he knows that all he needs to do is hold the paper up to a heat source—a warm light bulb—and the writing will reappear as faint brown letters.

Pretty mysterious, huh?

Is It Comic? No, It's "Serial"

Life is "seriously serial" in some comic strips . . . the ones that, rather than being funny, depict ongoing dramas. Your child probably sees his own everyday life as another high drama. So why doesn't your child draw a strip about his life? He doesn't need great artistic talent—stick figures will do if need be. All he has to do is depict, in four or five boxes (or more, if he pretends that it's Sunday!), the events of the day, or one event.

Here's a chance to let his fantasies loose, too. If he chooses, instead of an accurate rendition of today's highlight (or lowlight), he can depict life's events as he wishes they happened, or in a dramatically exaggerated version of the truth.

And if his life is so full of drama and events that he can't tell each day's story even in the space a Sunday strip would allow for, he can think "comic book" rather than "comic strip" and lengthen the tale accordingly.

O N E

MATERIALS

✐ Paper, pen or pencil

153

It Means What It Sounds Like

MATERIALS

✐ Paper, pen or pencil

Humpty Dumpty, in *Alice's Adventures in Wonderland*, said, "When I use a word, it means just what I choose it to mean—neither more nor less."

Most people don't twist words to mean something different than their usual meaning. It can create too much confusion. But writers over the years have invented words to mean exactly what the writers want them to. And some words—invented or otherwise—just sound like the things they're meant to.

Doesn't the word SLAM sound like just what it describes? It has a hard, harsh, sharp sound, like the sound of a door slamming or a book going slam on a table. The word HOOT, too, sounds a lot like what it's describing. And the word WHISPER is as soft and gliding and flowing—and sibilant—as an actual whisper.

Invent some words that sound like their meanings. Write them down. Start a "dictionary" of your invented words.

It's a Collyfluribus!

There are still a few parts of the world that haven't been fully explored—like the depths of the Amazon jungle or the heart of any deep woods. So it's still possible that explorers or scientists might discover a whole new kind of animal, bird, or fish.

What do you suppose such an animal might look like? Describe it. Draw a picture of it, if you'd like. What name would you give it? What do you imagine it might eat? What sound would it make? Where would it live—underground, or in the treetops, or in a cave, or where? What else can you think of to say about this new kind of animal?

It's fun to imagine, isn't it?

ONE
or more

MATERIALS

✎ None; or paper, pen or pencil, possibly crayons

I've "Bean" to Boston

T W O

or more

MATERIALS

✎ Popsicle sticks, beans, chairs or pillows or other objects suitable to use as obstacles.

For more than two players: Paper, pen or pencil

Here's a race that isn't won by being the fastest!

In this obstacle race, players must get from the start to the finish line on their knees, while holding a Popsicle stick on which are perched several beans, the same number to start with for each player. The winner is the player who reaches the finish line with the largest number of beans still on her Popsicle stick. The beans can be of any type, such as lima beans, coffee beans, or navy beans.

Players can race individually or as teams. In team play, keep track of each player's result and add up the team members' scores at the end. Team players returning to the start line should scoop up beans they dropped along the way so the next player starts with the right number.

Set up a variety of obstacles, an equal number in the path of both players (or teams)—chairs, throw pillows, boxes, and so on. Players must go around the obstacles, trying not to drop beans as they maneuver.

(Again, speed doesn't win this race. The number of beans left on the Popsicle stick does.)

Jessica Originals

Plain white tennis shoes—as long as they don't have a fashionable name attached somewhere—are relatively inexpensive, offer the opportunity for a challenging, fun after-school activity, and may even result in an end to your child's demands for a pair of Nikes! Here's how your child goes about turning a pair of plain white sneaks into a "Jessica Original":

Sketch pictures or designs in pencil on the canvas. When the design looks right, trace over the lines with indelible black marker. Fill in the picture or design with acrylic paint or indelible colored marker.

The result is unique and personalized. Your child will be proud to have created her own clothing design. And the other kids' parents will praise you to eternity if your child's nondesigner-shoes style catches on. You'll be a neighborhood hero if the other kids come to prefer their own $7 footwear to the fashionable shoes whose cost must be calculated on the same basis as a mortgage payment.

O N E

MATERIALS

Plain white sneakers, pencil, black indelible marker (such as a laundry marker), acrylic paint (or colored indelible marker)

Jeweled Egg Ornaments

MATERIALS

Egg, heavy darning needle, sequins, glitter, egg hangers (available at crafts shops), disinfectant, water, Elmer's Glue, two bowls

If you have a patient, steady-handed child, she can create some truly attractive ornaments. Here are instructions:

Shake the egg vigorously (without losing your grip on it!). Pierce both ends of the egg with a darning needle, and hold the egg over a bowl while you blow the contents out. Save the raw egg for scrambling or other cooking use. Be careful not to get any of the raw egg in your mouth. (Note to parent: If you are in doubt about your child's ability to keep the egg out of her mouth, take over for this step.)

Add some disinfectant to a bowl of water, and swish the egg through it, getting the solution inside the egg. Then rinse it out and put it aside to dry. When it's completely dried, coat it with glue to strengthen the shell. Three coats are recommended.

Now all you need to do is glue on the sequins and glitter, holding the egg carefully as you work. Allow the glue to dry, add the hanger, and hang it for all to see.

Jigsaw Books

You'll want to lend these puzzles to your friends to solve, but creating them is a job you can do alone.

O N E

First write a story on construction paper. Ideally you'll write the story yourself, but if not, you can retell a familiar story in your own words. Write on just one side of the paper. If you need more than one sheet of paper, they must all be different colors. (Important!) Number your pages.

MATERIALS

Several sheets of construction paper, each a different color; one sheet of lightweight cardboard for each sheet of construction paper you use; black fine-line marking pen; scissors; glue

Leave a margin all around the page. Glue each page to a piece of lightweight cardboard, printed-side up. Trim around the edges of the paper to fit the cardboard. (That's why you left the margins.) Cut the cardboard-backed paper into pieces in the manner of a jigsaw puzzle.

Now you have a jigsaw puzzle that tells a story instead of showing a picture. Since each page is a different color, you needn't worry about mixing the pages together; you know that the red pieces are all one page, the yellow pieces another page, and so forth. And since you've numbered the pages, you know the order in which to read them when you have the story reassembled.

You can have fun trying to put the story back together yourself, or you can give it to your friends and challenge them.

Jigsaw Valentines

MATERIALS

Red construction paper, black fine-line marker, scissors (beginner's scissors are okay), envelope

Next Valentine's Day, give valentines that are double fun! Cut as large a heart as you can out of a piece of red construction paper. Write your greeting, message, and signature on only one side of the paper. Then cut the heart into pieces with the scissors. (For a valentine to be given from one six-year-old to another, five or fifteen pieces might be a reasonable number; for a valentine to and from a twelve-year-old, one hundred might be a reasonable number.)

Put the pieces into an envelope and seal it so the pieces don't get lost.

The reason for writing your message on one side only is so that the recipient knows which side of the paper goes up and which goes down. You want to baffle the recipient but not totally frustrate him.

Join the Circus— at Home

What child hasn't at some time wanted to leave town and travel with the circus? Well, I can't help with the leaving town part, but any kid can learn to be a clown! And if he gets very good at it, he might be entertaining at little kids' birthday parties by the time he's fourteen or so. That isn't exactly Ringling Brothers, but it is putting on a performance for a very appreciative audience!

ONE

MATERIALS

✐ Makeup, silly clothes

Of course a clown has to do more than dress up in baggy or ridiculous clothes with a wildly made-up face. Your child will need to either juggle, do magic tricks, or develop a silly routine, like the famous clown routine of trying to sweep your shadow away with a broom.

But clowning is an art, like any other, and so it requires a lot of practice: practice in applying makeup and practice in your young clown's routine or performance. Can you think of a better way to spend time after school than being silly in front of a mirror . . . so that you can be good enough to one day perform for an adoring public?

Keep a Straight Face

THREE
or more

MATERIALS

🖋 None

Here's another try-not-to-laugh contest (see Stare Down, page 303), but this one's quite different. One of the players is picked to be the MC, who has two chances to make each of the other players either break up in laughter or at least crack a grin. He does this by posing a problem to them—a funny problem, for which they have to provide a seemingly serious answer. The MC's "problem" might be, "My hippopotamus ate my bathtub and I haven't bathed in a week," or "My dog dug up an emu egg and now the emu is sitting on the house, trying to hatch it."

The Advisor listens to the problem, then has to give some sort of solution for it. The MC gets two tries with each player, posing two different problems to each one. Any player who laughs, snickers, giggles, grins, guffaws, or otherwise fails to keep a totally straight face loses. All players who succeed are winners.

When the MC has had a chance at cracking up all the other players the round is over and somebody else has a chance to be MC, starting all over again.

Keeping It Uniform

Students at many private schools have worn uniforms to school for years. Now there's a trend toward uniforms in some public schools. Regardless of where you stand on the issue, there's a chance your child might one day be required to wear a uniform to school—if she doesn't have to already.

What will the uniform consist of? Will it be something sharp . . . or something geeky? Wouldn't your child like the chance to design her own uniform?

She may never get to wear it, but here's a chance for her to at least design one. All she needs is paper and crayons or fine-line markers, and she can design a school uniform, right down to the colors.

O N E
or more

MATERIALS

✎ Crayons or fine-line markers, paper

163

Kick the Can

MATERIALS

✐ One tin can

Decide on boundaries and where Base and Prison are. Base is a tin can, best located in the middle of a large open area so that it's possible to rush toward the can from any direction. Prison should be near Base but not so near as to impede a rush toward Base.

Choose an It, who covers his eyes and counts to 100 while the others hide. After reaching 100, It calls, "Ready or not, here I come!" and begins searching for the others. When It finds a hiding player, both run toward Base. If It gets there first, he jumps over the can, crying, "Over the can on [name of discovered player]." That player must now go to Prison.

If the discovered player reaches Base first, however, he kicks the can and yells, "[Name of player] kicked the can." All players in prison are then freed. Return the can to its original location.

If a player hiding near Base sees a clear field between there and himself, he can also run to Base, kick the can, yell, and free all the prisoners.

It gets out of being It only by imprisoning all the other players, a difficult task. Frequently the game continues till it's just too dark to keep playing.

Kids Can Cook Too

How would your child like to write a cookbook? He can. All he has to do is collect kid-friendly recipes and type them (preferably, or else write neatly) into cookbook format. If you have a computer, he can print out multiple copies and distribute them to his friends.

He might—though this is only a suggestion—divide the cookbook into two sections: recipes kids can cook themselves and recipes kids love to eat (but that are beyond the ability of most kids to cook on their own).

He can collect the recipes from his friends, their parents, relatives, neighbors, and friends of the family. This will probably involve taking the information down in pen while interviewing people either in person or over the phone. Later he can type it up for the cookbook.

If he can make copies of the book, by either running it out of a computer or making photocopies, he can even sell them, lemonade-stand-style.

O N E

MATERIALS

Paper, pen, typewriter or computer

165

Kings in the Corner

T W O
to four

MATERIALS

✐ Deck of cards
(bridge/poker)

Deal seven cards to each player and place the remainder of the deck facedown in a draw pile on the table. Turn four cards up, placing each one on one side of the draw pile. These are your corner cards. Play now proceeds clockwise, beginning with the player to the left of the dealer.

Each player draws one card from the draw pile and adds it to his hand, then plays one of the cards in his hand onto one of the corner cards if he can. Permissible play is to lay off the next-lowest number on a card of opposite color. In other words, if the four corner cards are a red Queen, a black 10, a black 7, and a red 4, the only playable cards are a black Jack, a red 9, a red 6, and a black 3. There is one exception: A player holding a King may play it on any corner at any time during his turn.

If a player cannot play, the turn passes to the next player right away. If a player does have a playable card, plays it, and has another playable card, he may immediately play that. He continues till he has no playable cards. Play then passes to the next player.

Play continues till one player runs out of cards. He is then declared the winner.

Knowledge Tag

Knowledge Tag is a variant on Stoop Tag . . . which really should be called Squat Tag, since in that game it's by squatting that players avoid getting tagged. But in Knowledge Tag, as you squat to avoid being tagged, you have to call out an example of the category that's been decided on before the round started.

TWO
or more (and the more, the merrier)

If the category for this round is Native American Tribes, then a player who squats must call out a tribe: "Iroquois!" Once Iroquois has been called, it may not be called again by any player.

MATERIALS

✐ None

A player who is tagged becomes It, just as in the conventional version of Tag. Players become It if they fail to squat quickly enough, if they fail to call out a valid example of the category that has been agreed on, or if they call out an example that's been used already.

Other possible categories include Countries, States, Colleges, Foods, Baseball Teams, Breeds of Dog, Presidents of the United States, Bodies of Water, Words Beginning with W, or Characters in Books.

MATERIALS

Leaves of various sizes, preferably ones with a fairly oval shape (as opposed to, for instance, oak leaves); glue; small buttons and/or sequins and/or seeds; very small twigs (perhaps from a bush rather than from a tree); construction paper or cardboard

Leaf People

Have fun with leaves by creating leaf people. How? Easy. In the middle of a piece of construction paper, glue a large, oval leaf that will serve as your leaf person's body. Above it, glue a smaller oval leaf that will be the head. Make a face on the head by gluing two eyes and a nose. These can be sequins, very small buttons, or seeds (either found in nature or on the kitchen spice shelf, such as sesame seeds). Form a mouth either by laying down a line of glue that forms a "smile mouth" and sprinkling seeds onto it or by gluing an appropriate-sized twig into place.

You may have another idea for the features, such as making the eyes from very thin slices of a carrot tip. (The tip will provide smaller and more appropriate-sized eyes than the broader middle of the carrot.)

Use twigs again for the arms and legs. Cornsilk and celery strings are two possibilities for hair, though hair isn't a necessity.

A Letter to a Friend

Do you have a friend in another town or state? When's the last time you wrote him a letter?

For some kids, the hardest part of writing a letter is deciding what to say. But it shouldn't be difficult—just pretend you're talking to your friend. If he were sitting in your room, what would you want to tell him? What has happened to you since you saw him last?

Have you gotten any particularly good grades on a test or report card? Had a funny substitute teacher? Won a Little League game? Gotten a medal in Scouts? Gone on a camping trip? Gone to the beach? Gone to a skating rink? Gotten an award? Gotten into a fight? Gotten a new pet? Made a new friend? Moved? Stayed up extra-late? Seen something funny? Tell your friend . . . the same as you would if he were right there with you.

O N E

MATERIALS

✐ Paper, pen or typewriter

169

You and your child or
your spouse and your
child or all three

MATERIALS

✏ None

Long Ago—When You Were a Kid

Agreat sense of closeness is fostered when you and your child sit down and have a chat on a personal level. And one of the greatest kinds of chat for letting kids see their parents as people is a conversation about your (or your spouse's) childhood. What were things like when you were a kid?

What scared you as a child? Were you afraid of thunder, or spiders, or mice, or snakes? What else was unpleasant? Did you hate liver too? And broccoli? Did you hate going to the dentist, or to the doctor for a shot? (But you went all the same, just like your child has to, right?)

What were your greatest pleasures? What were your happiest times? How did you celebrate holidays? How did your parents punish you?

Let your child ask the questions, but you can steer him in certain directions. And give honest answers (unless they're truly inappropriate for him to hear). If he learns to see you as a person who once was a kid, childhood may seem a tad less difficult for him to deal with. You had the same problems he did—or maybe worse ones. And you got through it okay.

Magazine Letter Scavenger Hunt

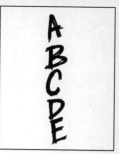

Here's a scavenger hunt that doesn't require your child and his sibling(s) or friend(s) to go out of the house on a rainy day or even to go looking through the house. They'll have a good time without ever getting up from where they're sitting.

or more, with parental involvement

Have the kids each write the letters from A through Z down the left side of their respective sheets of paper. (They'll probably need more than one each.) Now each player goes through a magazine or two, looking for pictures of items that start with each letter of the alphabet. When he finds a useful picture, he writes the item next to its letter, as well as the page of the magazine on which he found it. Many pictures will offer multiple possibilities. Just from a picture of a person, for instance, your child can fulfill many letters by writing down the various body parts that show.

MATERIALS

✐ Pens, paper, magazines

Some letters may be impossible to find. The winner is either the first child to complete the alphabet . . . or, if no one does, the player who has found the most letters when you, the parent, call time.

Magazine Scavenger Hunt

TWO
or more, with
parental involvement

MATERIALS

Magazines (more
magazines than
there are players)
with lots of
pictures
(including ads) in
them, nonplaying
person (such as a
parent), paper,
pen or pencil,
scissors (ideally,
a pair for each
player, though
this isn't
essential)

This one's related to the previous activity. You, the parent, need to prepare by making up a list of pictures of things to be found in the pages of magazines. These might include a stop sign, a barn, a body of water, a small boy, an office building, a milk carton, a police officer, and other such items. You need to make one copy of the list for each player. An ideal list would contain perhaps fifteen or twenty items.

At a signal, each player takes a magazine and starts looking through it for as many pictures as she can find that fit the items on the list (but only one of each item). She cuts or tears each picture out as she finds it.

After a set amount of time—perhaps twenty minutes—decided on in advance, the parent calls, "Time," and all the players stop searching through the magazines. At that point, the player who has found the largest number of items on her list is the winner.

Alternative play: Each player is given a different list so that players are not looking for the same items.

Magic Garden of Jupiter

Even if your child is old enough to engage in this activity alone, you may want to join in for the sheer fun of it!

To 2 tablespoons of liquid bluing, add enough salt that the mixture is a thick, grainy liquid. Put a charcoal briquette or piece of coal in the middle of a disposable aluminum pie plate and slowly drizzle the salt-and-bluing mixture onto it, trying to keep most of it on top of the briquette rather than letting it run into the pie pan. Now add a little water in the bottom of the pan. Be sure to pour around the briquette rather than onto it so that you don't wash the salt-and-bluing mixture off the briquette.

Within an hour, your Magic Garden will begin to assume mesmerizing fantastic growths, spires that spurt up, and all manner of shapes.

Cautions: Because your Magic Garden's growth pattern is unpredictable, and because it can damage fine furniture, don't set it up where it can do harm if it spills over. Because your Magic Garden is fragile and should not be disturbed, don't leave it where it might be bumped, and don't touch it.

O N E
or more

Safety reminder:
Liquid bluing can be harmful if ingested.

MATERIALS

- 2 tablespoons liquid bluing, salt, disposable aluminum pie pan, piece of coal or charcoal briquette, water

- Optional: Food coloring

173

Make a Distinctive Vase

MATERIALS

Large jar, black paint, paintbrush, glue, elbow macaroni, newspaper to work over

Your child can make a vase in which you (or Grandma or a favorite aunt) will be proud to display flowers. Here's how: First paint the outside of a jar with black paint, covering the jar completely. Let it dry.

When it's totally dry, spread glue over one side of the jar and apply the elbow macaroni to it, not covering every inch of it but letting some of the black paint show. When that side is finished, work on the other half, handling it carefully so that you don't dislodge any of the elbows that are glued in place.

Make a Door Nameplate

The messy condition of your child's room leaves no doubt as to the age of the inhabitant. But he'd still glow with pride of ownership if there were no doubt as to who, exactly, it is that lives there.

Why not have him draw a nameplate with JEFF'S ROOM in bright colors, perhaps with a design in each of the four corners? This can be an abstract design— a squiggle or zigzag or curlicue—or it can be a picture of something that he relates to—baseballs in two corners and bats in two corners, or a different car in each corner, or dinosaurs, or fish.

I'm not, however, claiming that pride of ownership will encourage him to clean his room!

O N E

MATERIALS

- Poster board (preferably) or cardboard, paint or crayons or colored marking pens, two-sided poster tape, scissors

175

Make a Pinwheel!

MATERIALS

✐ Piece of typing paper or construction paper, scissors (beginner's scissors are okay), pencil or wooden ruler or small stick, thumbtack or pushpin

✂ Optional: Crayons or paint and/or glue and glitter

Cut the paper into a square. If it's 9-by-12-inch construction paper, you can cut it into a 9-inch square; if it's 8½-by-11-inch typing paper, you can cut it into an 8½-inch square.

Put your scissors at each of the four corners and cut toward the middle, but stop just short of the middle. (If it helps you to cut a straight line, draw a line from each corner to the corner diagonally opposite it. Then just cut along those lines—again, stopping just short of the middle.)

Having made the cuts, you now have a square that's divided into four "almost" triangles. Take the right-hand corner of each of the four triangles and bend it toward the middle. (Do not crease the pinwheel.) Holding those four corners together in place, push a thumbtack or pushpin through the four corners, and the center below them, into a pencil, a small, thin piece of wood such as a wooden ruler, or a small stick. Do not push the tack all the way in. You want to leave room so that the pinwheel will rotate when the wind catches it; in other words, you need to leave it loose. Wiggle the paper around a little to loosen it, if necessary

Now all you need is a windy day, and you're set to have fun.

Make a Themed Collage

Is your daughter crazy for horses? Is your son a real nut for boats or sports cars? They can decorate the walls of their rooms with collages featuring nothing but those horses, boats, or whatever . . . floats their boats.

It's a simple enough procedure—you know the concept behind a collage: First cut out pictures (cutting right around the image of the dog, kitten, sports figure, and so on, rather than cutting out a square that includes the central image). Next, artfully arrange the pictures so that in at least some cases, part of one image overlaps part of another. When you're happy with the final result, glue the pictures down permanently.

Gluing the pictures onto construction paper has the advantage of giving you a colorful background that will show through in any spots that aren't covered by a picture. On the other hand, gluing them onto cardboard will give them greater longevity.

He can start saving appealing images now; when he has enough clowns, enough sunsets, or enough happy faces for a new collage, he's ready to make the next one.

MATERIALS

Cardboard or construction paper; scissors; glue; pictures from magazines, greeting cards, postcards, and/or photographs

O N E

MATERIALS

✐ Four cylindrical
oatmeal (or grits
or raisin)
containers
(preferably with
their lids) or four
or five coffee cans
(less desirable),
construction
paper, paint,
scissors, glue

Make a Totem Pole

You'll need to save four oatmeal (or
similar cylindrical) containers in
advance for this. Coffee cans can be
substituted if necessary. (If you use coffee
cans, a parent needs to first make sure
there are no sharp edges.)

Cut a piece of construction paper (or
two the same color, if needed) for each
container, and draw a face on it. Then
glue it in place on the container. Glue the
containers one on top of the other. Let the
glue dry thoroughly.

You don't have to attempt an authentic
Native American look. Any kind of face
will do.

178

Make a Wishing Tree

There's really nothing magical about a wishing tree. However, kids invest magical properties in many things—so why not a branch of a tree with colored paper stuck to it?

Break off a branch of a tree or a part of a bush, preferably one with quite a few smaller branches or twigs, and "plant" it in a large can or jar half filled with sand or dirt or potting soil.

Create leaves by cutting them out of construction paper. They all can be green, you may opt for autumn colors for the sake of brightness, or they can be pink, purple, chartreuse, or any other color you like. This is your creation, and realism is not a requirement.

Write all your Very Important Wishes—and even your minor ones, if the major ones aren't too plentiful—each on a separate leaf. Save the leftover leaves for future wishes. Tack the wishing leaves on the tree, wishing real hard as you push in the pushpins or thumbtacks.

As you make new wishes, write them on leaves and tack them up. As your wishes come true, take those leaves off— with a feeling of great satisfaction!

O N E
or more or the
whole family

MATERIALS

✐ Tree branch, construction paper, scissors, pen or pencil, large can or jar half filled with sand or dirt or potting soil, pushpins or thumbtacks

179

Make Bookplates

O N E

MATERIALS

- Paper (white typing paper or construction paper), crayons or marking pens, glue, scissors

Lending books is often a losing proposition. You're lucky if you get them back at all, never mind what condition they come back in. And with kids, there is often a dispute: "That's my copy of Winnie the Pooh." "No, it's mine!"

One way to solve disputes . . . and ease a book's return to its rightful owner . . . is to put a bookplate inside the front cover of every book. A bookplate can be as simple as a small piece of paper with a basic message: PROPERTY OF SUE SMITH or THIS BOOK BELONGS TO JOHN ANDERSEN or LINDA LEDERER'S BOOK, with the words written in ink on plain white paper. On the other hand, it can be a thing of beauty, with illustrations, with fancy lettering, with various colors being used, and with the whole thing being done up on colorful paper.

Making extra-fancy illustrated bookplates for a slew of books can be daunting . . . but then again, nobody said you had to get it all done in one rainy afternoon. Either way, you're helping protect your valuable collection . . . and minimizing disputes with friends.

Make Masks . . . Just for Fun—1

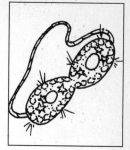

Making masks is a great activity to do with friends because it's noncompetitive, but it's also quite suitable for the solo child.

To make construction paper masks, cut a piece of bright-colored, preferably pastel construction paper in half so that you have two pieces, 6 by 9 inches. You can make a mask out of each piece. Fold one of these pieces in half so that the two short sides meet, and draw an unfinished oval on the folded sheet. The side where the oval is incomplete is the side where the fold is; thus, when you cut the oval out and unfold it, you have two "almost" ovals that will cover your eyes, connected by a strip over the bridge of your nose. Now cut an eyehole in the middle of each oval.

Decorate the masks with crayons or paint; you can also apply decorations such as glitter, feathers, sequins, or buttons.

Hold the mask on your face with either a very large rubber band or yarn or ribbon, stapling whichever you use to each side of the mask.

O N E
or more

MATERIALS

- Construction paper, rubber bands or ribbons or yarn, crayons and/or paints

- Optional: Glitter, feathers, sequins, buttons, or other decorations

181

Make Masks . . .
Just for Fun—2

O N E
or more

MATERIALS

🖉 White paper plates, rubber bands or ribbons or yarn, crayons and/or paints

✂ Optional: Glitter, feathers, sequins, buttons, or other decorations

In addition to construction paper masks, you can also make masks out of plain white paper plates. Hold the plate in front of your face (with the top toward your face and the bottom facing out) and, using a crayon (not a pencil or other sharp instrument!), make a mark where each of your eyes is. Then cut an eye-sized area around each of the two crayon marks. Do the same for your mouth.

Now draw eyes around the eyeholes, lips around the mouth hole, and a nose; add rosy cheeks, hair, eyebrows (scowling? raised in surprise? bushy? thin and delicate?), or any other specifics that appeal to you.

Hold the mask on your face by one of the methods described in the previous activity—using either a rubber band or yarn or ribbon.

These masks can be worn for Halloween, for putting on shows, or just for fun.

Make Old-Fashioned Paper Dolls

First draw one or more dolls on white poster board. They should be wearing just underwear, if anything. Cut them out.

Now draw different outfits for the dolls. Each outfit should be the right size for the dolls and should have ½-inch tabs extending out all around it. You'll keep each item of clothing in place on the dolls by bending the tabs back behind the dolls.

You can give your doll, or dolls, as many different outfits as you want.

O N E
or more

MATERIALS

⊘ Poster board, heavyweight white typing paper, crayons, scissors

Make the Connection

MATERIALS

✎ None

The premise and rules of this game are simple: Player 1 names two unrelated items, and Player 2 has to invent a connection between them. Then they trade places, and Player 2 names two items, leaving it up to Player 1 to make the connection.

The connections can be realistic or fanciful. Suppose Player 1 says, "Peacock eggs and a TV camera." Player 2 might say, "The TV station sends the cameraman to take pictures of the eggs and show them hatching," "When the eggs hatch, the peacock's feathers can be used as a feather duster to clean the lens of the TV camera," or even "A TV cameraman is taking pictures at the circus, and he's hungry, so he eats a peacock egg."

This is not a competitive game, so neither player is attempting to win by stumping the other player. The fun lies in trying to connect two unrelated items; so don't make it too easy on each other. It's no stretch to connect a child and a book, or a robin and a bush. Make it tough on the other player and make him exercise his creative "muscles."

184

Making Book— Literally!

Your child is going to make a special kind of book—one with cloth pages— with your help at the beginning and end of the project. First cut four or five pieces of plain white (or off-white) cloth into rectangles approximately 12 by 16 inches. Old white shirts or a sheet will work; heavier cloth is better; light canvas is ideal. Stack the rectangles on top of each other, lining them up evenly, and sew a seam right down the middle (from one 16-inch side to the other). This is easier to do on a sewing machine than by hand.

Now your child draws on each page with crayons. He can draw all the pictures on a particular subject or draw pictures that tell a story in sequence; or the pictures may be unrelated to each other.

When he's finished, it's your turn to get involved again, preserving the drawings by pressing each page with a warm iron. Protect the page, the iron, and the pages below by putting one pressing cloth (an old towel or rag) above the page and another below.

Your child now has a unique book . . . that he made himself!

O N E
with parental help

MATERIALS

✏ Plain white cloth, needle and thread or sewing machine, crayons, iron, pressing rag such as an old towel

185

Many Happy Returns . . . and Exchanges

MATERIALS

✐ None

Birthday (and other) presents often come with gift tags that read, "Many happy returns!" An odd phrase, but one that is most appropriate when you stop to think where so many birthday gifts wind up—that is, at the Returns and Exchanges counter!

The first player leads off with, "On the day after my birthday, I returned _____." He can fill in any gift he wants . . . but why choose something as mundane as "a sweater"? How about "a woolly mammoth"? The second player adds an item and repeats the first one: "On the day after my birthday, I returned a purple slingshot and a woolly mammoth." The third player continues in the same way: "On the day after my birthday, I returned some cola-flavored jelly, a purple slingshot, and a woolly mammoth."

Keep going around—you can play with just two players (going back and forth), with a large crowd, or with any number in between. Any player who messes up is out of the game. The last one left wins.

186

Map Games— Stump Your Parents

Having a large map on the wall of a frequently used room—such as the kitchen or family room—is a stealthy way to sneak information into your child's mind without him realizing it. If his chair at the kitchen table faces a large map of the United States or the world, he's likely to learn what states the Mississippi River traverses, which states have four pretty straight lines for borders, or what European countries border the Mediterranean.

One game that will make studying the map seem more like fun and less like extended school hours is Stump Your Parents. To play, your child studies the map, ascertains some fact or another, then poses a question to you to see if you know the answer. Quick . . . what's the capital of Holland? Can you name all the countries that share a common border with France? Where does the Missouri River terminate? What's the capital of Montana?

He's likely to show you up . . . and to feel pretty smug about it. Good! That ought to send him back to the map to learn some more "stealth information."

Who's feeling smug now?

ONE
or more

MATERIALS

✐ Large map

Marble Roll

MATERIALS

✐ Marbles, empty coffee can (or a smaller can if need be)

Here's yet another game that's fun either solo or in competition. The premise is ridiculously simple; achieving the goal is remarkably less so.

Place a clean, empty can on its side on the floor. (Parental alert: Check the can for sharp edges first.) A wood floor is better than a carpeted floor. Stand perhaps 3 feet away, holding a marble. Roll the marble at the can, trying to get it inside. (Rather than having to chase after the same marble after every roll, it's easier to start with a handful of them, retrieving them all after you've rolled them all.)

Can you score? It's not as easy as it looks! Even though the can is much larger than the marble, there isn't that large an area of the can that is flat to the floor, and the challenge is much tougher than it appears.

No, it's not impossible. But it sure isn't easy, either!

Match or Pay

Here's a solo game of pure chance that—in common with most solitaires—you'll find you lose at far more often than you win. From a deck of cards, take an Ace, 2, 3, 4, 5, and 6. (The color and suit are irrelevant.) Shuffle them. For the purpose of this game, an Ace has the value of 1. Now divide twenty poker chips (or paper clips or pennies or any other similar item) into two piles of ten each. One pile is yours; the other pile is "the bank." Put your pile of chips in front of you, and put the bank pile off to the side somewhere. You're now ready to start playing.

O N E

Roll the die. Now turn the top card over. If they match—that is, if you've rolled a five on the die and the card you've turned over is also a 5—take a chip from the bank. If they don't match, though, you have to pay the bank a chip. Return the card to the "deck" of six cards and shuffle again. Repeat the process.

Continue till you "break the bank" (get all the bank's chips) and win or "go bankrupt" (pay all your chips to the bank) and lose.

MATERIALS

- A die, six cards (Ace through 6), twenty poker chips or pennies or paper clips or walnuts or similar item (even scraps of paper will do)

189

Match or Pay— Odds and Evens

MATERIALS

One die, six cards (Ace through 6), twenty poker chips or pennies or paper clips or walnuts or similar items (even scraps of paper will do)

If the preceding game proves too frustrating for you—and admittedly your chances of winning are very slim, as with most solitaire games—here's a version of the game in which you have a much better chance of winning.

Prepare for the game in exactly the same manner, and then proceed to play in the same manner, with this one big exception: You don't have to match the number on the die to the number on the card. You only have to match odds to odds and evens to evens. That is, if the die comes up an odd number—1, 3, or 5— you need to turn over an odd-numbered card—Ace, 3, or 5—in order to win. If you succeed, take a chip from the bank. Similarly, if you roll a 2, 4, or 6, your card needs to be a 2, 4, or 6.

As you can see, you have a 50 percent chance of winning this game. Though it's by no means a sure thing, at least the odds aren't stacked against you.

Measuring in Tony Feet

It's hard for a child to relate to feet and inches. After all, they're arbitrary measurements. Whose feet? Not his!

ONE
or more

MATERIALS

✐ None; or paper, pen or pencil

But what if measurements were in "Tony feet" (or whatever your child's name is). Now that's a measurement he can understand. Instead of his room being 10 by 10 feet, suddenly it's much larger—maybe even 22 by 22 feet—and each of those "feet" is a "real foot"—his foot!

All he has to do is pace heel to toe across whatever space he wants to measure. How big is his room? How long is the hallway? How far is it from the front door to the sidewalk? How big is the backyard? If you live in an apartment building, how long is your hallway? What's the size of the lobby downstairs? How many feet is it from your apartment door to the elevator or garbage chute, or any other feature in your building?

He can write down the results if he wants to. And if he does, he can compare them with the same measurements a year later. If the living room measures noticeably fewer "Tony feet" this year than last, that's proof that he's growing . . . feet included.

Miniature "Christmas Trees"

MATERIALS

Large pine cone, small sheet of aluminum foil, jar lid slightly larger than pine cone's base, glue, paint and/or tinsel and/or sequins and/or glitter

Here's an easy Christmas decoration your child can make, even at an early age. He starts with the lid of a jar, making sure it's clean and then covering it with aluminum foil. Now he glues the base of a pine cone to the top of the foil-covered lid.

Finally, he decorates the cone. For this, he can use paint, glitter, sequins, or any combination of those. In addition, if he wants, he can use a little tinsel, though this should be used very sparingly.

The tree is finished and ready to grace his desk, his night table, the dining room table, or your family room.

Mirror Drawing

Here's a challenge that's difficult but fun. Your child can do it alone or with friends, laughing at the results that each child produces. Here's what to do: Put a piece of paper in front of you. Now hold a mirror in the hand you don't write with (your left if you're a rightie, your right if you're a lefty). Looking only in the mirror and not at the paper in front of you, try to write your name or, better yet, a whole sentence. Now draw a stick figure or a house or, better yet, draw a whole picture.

It's not easy, is it? And the results are laughable . . . but we can all use a good laugh!

 O N E

MATERIALS

✐ Paper, pen or pencil, handheld mirror

193

Mirror Image

MATERIALS

Sheet of white typing paper or construction paper, crayons, magazine picture of a face (preferably fairly large in size), scissors, glue

For this particular brand of fun, you'll first need to find a picture of a face in a magazine. You want to find one that's looking at the camera straight on, not in profile. Cut it out, then cut it in half right up the middle, from the chin to the top of the head. Now glue it down on a sheet of white paper, leaving plenty of space to the side so that you can complete the picture.

And that's just what the rest of this pastime consists of, that is, taking your crayons and trying to draw the other side of the face so that it matches as closely as possible. Can you match the other half of the nose or mouth? Will your eye be the same shape, size, and color as the one that's already there? How closely can you match the skin tone?

If the results are more laughable than artistic, don't fret. That's the usual result of this fun pastime.

Mirror Tic-Tac-Toe

Just as in Mirror Drawing (the previous activity), you won't look at the paper except in the mirror. But this is a game for two people.

Play tic-tac-toe without ever looking at the paper directly. Further complicating matters, whatever square you put your pencil down on is the square you must draw your X or O in. If you set it down in the wrong square, because you're turned around from using only the mirror to guide your pencil, that's unfortunate, but you're committed. The only exception is, of course, if you put your pencil down in a square that already has a mark in it. But then you have to lift your pencil up again before putting it down again; you may not just slide it across to the square you meant to aim for.

MATERIALS

✐ Handheld mirror, paper, pens or pencils

Mirror Walk

MATERIALS

✐ Handheld mirror

Give your child a handheld mirror and suggest he hold it horizontally, around stomach level, and walk around the house while looking down into the mirror (and keeping half an eye on the floor so that he doesn't trip over that truck you've been asking and asking him to pick up and put away).

The sensations are surreal; his feet are moving along the familiar living room rug, but the mirror makes the eyes feel as though the surface being walked on ought to be rough stucco. Stepping over light fixtures or the lintels of doorways also makes for odd feelings.

Despite the simplicity of the activity, it's fun. It won't take up a whole afternoon, but it's a great break on a day when he takes almost all the time before dinner to do homework and then looks for a quick activity before you call him to the table.

Mirror-Echo Name

Your child can make an interesting design to hang on his wall, and one that's personalized. Here's how he does it:

Fold a piece of construction paper in half and put it down in front of you with the fold to the bottom. Write your name (first only or first and last) in block outline capital letters, with the bottoms of the letters resting on the fold.

Now cut out the letters, being careful to not cut the bases, where the fold is. Unfold, and you have your name with its mirror image echoed below. Glue the result penciled-side down to a contrasting-colored sheet of construction paper.

O N E

MATERIALS

✐ Two sheets of construction paper (in contrasting colors), pencil, scissors, glue

Mix 'n' Match Proverbs

O N E
or more

MATERIALS

✐ Paper, pen or
pencil

Take the beginning of a proverb . . . and finish it with the end of another. What have you got? "The early bird gathers no moss." "An apple a day is worth two in the bush."

Your turn.

And when you're finished playing mix 'n' match proverbs, tacking on the end of one proverb to the beginning of another, try writing totally new endings to old proverbs. "Variety is . . ." ". . . the spice of life," according to the old proverb—but maybe you would finish it in another way? "A penny saved is . . ." Is what? Write your own finish to as many proverbs as you can.

198

Mixies

This is silly fun for the younger set. To prepare—and this part is best done by a parent—search out at least five and preferably more magazine pictures of people who are recognizable types . . . such as a firefighter, a cheerleader, a great-grandma, Santa Claus, a conservatively dressed businessman, a plumber or mechanic, a basketball player, a woman executive, a glitzily attired singer, and any other distinct types you can find, reasonably close in size to each other. Glue each picture to the cardboard, and cut across each one at the neck and again at the waist.

Now comes the fun for your child as he puts the pictures back together . . . deliberately wrongly, with Santa's head on the singer's body over the cheerleader's legs, or the firefighter's head on the businessman's body over the basketball player's legs.

Be prepared for repeated choruses of "Mom! Look at this!"

ONE
or more, with parental help the first time

MATERIALS

⌁ Pictures from magazines, scissors, glue, lightweight cardboard or old file folders

199

Monkey in the Middle

THREE

MATERIALS

✏ Ball

Monkey in the Middle is a throwing and catching game. Two people stand a reasonable distance from each other to throw and catch a rubber ball or tennis ball or similar type ball with some ease but not absolute certainty of catching it. The third person, the monkey, stands more or less midway between the two and tries to intercept the ball.

In some geographic areas, if the monkey catches the ball, she replaces the person who should have caught it; that person now becomes the monkey. In other parts of the country, it is the person who threw the ball who gets penalized and has to become the monkey.

There is no formal end to the game; it's over when everyone decides it's time to play something else.

Monogram Wall Decoration

In pencil, draw your initials fairly large on the poster board or cardboard or tagboard. When you're satisfied that the initials are all the same size, and neatly drawn, cut them out. Lay out the toothpicks around the edges of your initials so that you know how many you need to completely border the letters.

Choose two colors of paint. One, for the letters, might be a bright color you like, or a variation of the color on your bedroom walls (if they're not white), such as a deep blue if you have light blue walls. The other, for the toothpicks, should be a deeper color, perhaps even black; or it could be white if your walls aren't white.

Now paint one side of the toothpicks with the color you've selected for them, and put them aside to dry. While they dry, paint the letters with the color you've chosen for them. When the toothpicks are dry, turn them over and paint them on the other side.

When everything is quite dry, glue the toothpicks in place. (You may need to cut some toothpicks with a scissors to make them fit on the short sides of letters. Parental help is suggested to avoid splinter hazard.)

MATERIALS

Poster board or cardboard or tagboard, wooden toothpicks, glue, paint and paintbrush, scissors, pencil with eraser, newspaper to work over

Mosaic Nameplate

O N E

MATERIALS

Five sheets of construction paper (one preferably pastel or white and four in different colors), glue, pencil

Your child can create a colorful nameplate for the door of his room. The results are bright; the process is pretty easy. Here's how:

Start by writing your name in block outline letters on a sheet of construction paper, preferably white or pastel. Draw the letters as large as you can and still fit your whole name on one sheet, using pencil in case you need to erase and start over, for example, if you run out of paper before running out of letters.

Now you need to tear up the other sheets of construction paper—perhaps four different colors—into little bits. Carefully applying glue to one letter at a time, cover the glued areas with different-colored bits of torn paper.

Mother, May I?

Mother

Choose one player to be Mother. The others line up side by side, facing Mother across some distance. The object is to be the first player to cross the imaginary line on which Mother stands. Players may move only with Mother's permission, taking only as many steps, and as large a step, as Mother permits. The three sizes of step are baby steps (putting the heel of the advancing foot to the toe of the stationary foot), regular steps, and giant steps (strides as long as the player can manage).

Mother calls on any player and offers preliminary permission, specifying number of steps and size: "Mark, you may take two giant steps." But Mark must get confirmation: "Mother, may I?" Mother may say, "Yes, you may," or "No, you may not." If Mother says, "Yes, you may," Mark takes the steps; but if Mother says, "No, you may not," Mark must stay put. If he takes the steps without confirmation, he has to go all the way back to the starting line.

If you can inch forward without getting caught, you're a good player, not a bad sport. But if Mother catches you, it's back to the starting line for you!

GROUP
(and the larger, the better)

MATERIALS

✐ None

Mr. Hiss

ONE

MATERIALS

✎ Green pipe
cleaner, red felt
(preferable) or
red construction
paper, glue,
scissors, two
small black beads

Mr. Hiss is one snake who'll never bite you. With no fangs and a tongue made of felt or construction paper, he's harmless . . . and cute. Your child can have fun creating him, then enjoy looking at him as he lies around on top of her dresser or desk or bookcase.

A green pipe cleaner is the basis for the snake. Your child glues two very small beads at one end of the pipe cleaner, as eyes for Mr. Hiss. Next he cuts a forked tongue out of red felt or red construction paper and glues it below the eyes.

Easy, wasn't it? Your child might want to make a few more snakes to keep Mr. Hiss company.

My Friend Is a Real Dummy

Your child is about to get a new friend . . . and one who will talk back only when your child wants him to. That's because his new friend is a dummy . . . a real dummy. Your child can create a life-sized dummy using his own old clothes stuffed with rags or crumpled newspaper. Use strategically placed safety pins to hold the clothes closed, to anchor the stuffing in place, and to attach gloves to shirt, socks to pants. Affixing shoes can be a little more tricky: If your child isn't satisfied with socks alone, stuff the socks extra full and tie the shoes tightly. You'll need to use a long-sleeved shirt. A stuffed pair of gloves will give the appearance of hands.

For the face, stuff a paper bag or solid white or tan pillowcase. Draw features in paint, crayon, or marker. Glue yarn on top for hair, or perch a hat on the head.

Your child may opt to merely play with the dummy as if it's a life-sized doll, but how much better if he actually works up a ventriloquism act. He'll be the hit of the next birthday party or school talent show!

O N E

MATERIALS

✎ A set of your child's old clothes, rags or crumpled newspaper, a paper bag or a plain white or tan pillowcase, crayons or paint or markers, yarn, glue, safety pins

205

"My Room!"

MATERIALS

- Wood scraps, one large piece of wood, glue, marking pen

If you have a home woodworking shop, you probably have what your child needs to make a very distinctive nameplate for the door of his room. Start with cut ends of 1 inch and 2 inch lumber, each the right size for her to write one letter on. (But first, parents, please check for splinters and rough edges.)

Since the wood blocks are of random size, she can similarly write each letter in a different style. She may not know a Times-style typeface from a decorative type, or even serif from sans-serif. No matter. The point is this: If she's older than six or seven, she's probably realized by now that there's more than one "right" way to draw many of the letters in the alphabet. Here's a chance for her to experiment with forming each letter in a different style, though this isn't mandatory.

Now the letters need to be glued onto a piece of wood large enough to accommodate all of them. (If she's not old enough to handle that chore, the ball's back in your court.) And last, the wood needs to be nailed, glued, or otherwise hung on the door to her room.

And now there's no question about whose room it is!

Name Challenges

H ere are a few challenges involving names. Try these out on yourself and see how well you do. You can write your answers down if you want, though it's not necessary:

- Can you think of names that begin with each letter of the alphabet?
- Think of a two-letter name, a three-letter name, a four-letter name, a five-letter name, and so on. How high in letter count can you get?
- How many names can you think of that are also names of gemstones?
- How many names can you think of that are also flowers?
- What about names that are also animals or birds?

O N E
or more

MATERIALS

✏ None; or paper, pen or pencil

THOMAS!

ONE

MATERIALS

Paper, pencil

Name Games— Anagrams and Word Yields

There are various ways to have fun with your own name. You can play with your first name, your last name, or both, or use your middle name too.

To anagram your name(s), see if you can make a word or phrase by rearranging the letters in your first name, first and last, or first last and middle.

To play a word yield game, see how many words you can make out of the letters in your name(s). It's best to use both your names—or all three if you have a middle name—and your full first name, rather than your nickname. For instance, there's not much you can get out of TOM except TO, but THOMAS yields MOST, MAST, HOT, HAM, HAT, SAT, SOT, SHOT, TO, AT, MAT, SHAM, MATH, MASH, and SHOAT.

What can you get out of your name?

208

Name Games— Name Attributes

A nother kind of fun you can have with your name is to define yourself in terms of adjectives or phrases that begin with the respective letters of your name.

For instance, suppose your name is Tom. That might yield TALENTED, ON THE BALL, and MATURE. If your name is Anna, that could mean you're ABLE, NICE, NATURE-LOVING, and ADMIRABLE.

And what does your name say about you? Use your full name, your formal first name, or your nickname. Now, what can you say about your friends by assigning an adjective to each letter of their names?

ONE

MATERIALS

✐ Paper, pencil

Natural "Canvas" Painting

O N E
with parental help

MATERIALS

✎ Pine branch or small log, help from an adult with a bench saw; paint and paintbrush

Do you, Uncle Ed, or Aunt Jeannie own a bench saw? If so, you can cut a pine branch or small log at an angle so that you wind up with an elongated oval. Though it could be almost any size, why not aim for a "medallion" that's perhaps 1 inch thick and perhaps between 4 and 10 inches long. Okay, you've done your share of the work . . . now it's your child's turn to have fun. Here's how:

Prepare the surface by painting it with white primer. Paint the exposed wood of the center, but avoid getting paint on the rough bark. When it dries, paint a picture on the painted wood! What an unusual "canvas." And what a pretty place for a picture. The bark will frame your art in a rustic, very attractive way.

Won't Grandma love to have that sitting on her shelf . . . if you can bear to let it out of your own house, Mom!

Nature Bingo— Type I

For this activity, you, the parent, have to prepare in advance. Write a brief description of the items you want your child to find. These can be as simple as an elm leaf, an acorn, or a seed pod; or they can be more difficult, for an older child. Write each item on a Bingo-style card and then send your child out to find as many of the items as he can.

When he finds one, he crosses it off on his card—in pencil, which can be erased so the card can be reused.

If he's playing alone, his challenge is to see whether he can complete any of the lines and, if so, how many. Will he score Bingo? Will he make it a hat trick and score Bingo three times? Can he— gasp!—fill his whole card? If he's playing with a friend or sibling, give them different cards, if possible, and then see which of them can score the most Bingos.

Of course, they're on the honor system here.

O N E
or more

MATERIALS

✐ Bingo card(s) that you, the parent, have made up in advance; a pencil

Nature Bingo— Type II

O N E
or more

Instead of writing a description of an item in each of the twenty-five boxes on the Bingo card, glue a different type of leaf in each box. These can come from trees or bushes in your yard or in your neighborhood, but they must be leaves that your child can reach, such as leaves that are lying on the ground.

You may want to simplify the Bingo card in the interest of making all the leaves fit on one page, or for the sake of your child's age. You can make it look more like a tic-tac-toe board, with only three squares across and three down, instead of five by five.

In this version, he is obligated to collect a matching leaf for each leaf you have glued to the card. (The "card" in this case is probably going to be a full-sized sheet of cardboard.) He brings these back home with him and shows you. When you verify that he has indeed matched the leaf on his card, you lay the leaf he found on top of the card. For each line that he's covered completely, he gets credit for one Bingo.

Again, this can be played either as a solo challenge or competitively.

Neighborhood Scavenger Hunt

This scavenger hunt doesn't require the child to tote home old shoes or theatre ticket stubs; all he has to return with is notes on a list. But it's fun either for one child, trying to win by bringing back all the items, or for more than one child, trying to win by being the first to do so.

Interesting features of your area might include an oak tree with a dead limb, a rosebush in full bloom, a bee's nest, a house with a wraparound porch, a mailbox shaped like a locomotive, or a house painted lilac. Make a list of all these items.

Give your child a pencil and the list, and spell out boundaries for him: All these things can be found between Prairie Drive and Skyview Avenue, between 5th Street and 10th. Now he'll try to locate as many of the items as he can. You may, if you wish, give him a time limit. If there are two or more kids playing, each gets an identical list.

As he travels around your neighborhood in search of the listed items, he writes down the location of each when he finds them: "Yard of 364 Roosevelt" or "Corner of Elmdale and Hyacinth."

O N E
or more, with parental preparation

MATERIALS

✐ Paper, pen or pencil

213

The New 15¢ Coin

O N E
or more

MATERIALS

✐ Paper, pencil with eraser

No, Congress hasn't announced a new coin whose debut you missed reading about in the paper. There is no 15¢ piece. But if there were . . . what would it look like? That's a good question to pose to your child: How would you design a new coin? What would you depict on the obverse (front) and reverse (back) of a new coin? What color would it be; what metal would it be made of? How would it compare in size to our existing coins?

He can let his fancies range unfettered . . . perhaps his new coin will be square or pentagonal, or have a hole in the middle, or depict the flag or a flower instead of the bust of someone famous or the well-used eagle.

When he's done designing this "new coin," perhaps he'd like to redesign our existing coins . . . or maybe even figure out a whole new monetary system (decimal or otherwise). And how about designing some new postage stamps next?

New Style Building Blocks

Anyone can build with blocks. What can you build with? You can make a fort out of sofa cushions, a doll-sized teepee out of throw pillows, a tower out of plastic glasses, or a skyscraper out of poker chips. How about a building made of cartons? What can you construct out of checkers? Frying pans and kettles? What other "construction materials" do you have around the house?

Depending on the materials you use, your structures may be suitable just for fun, suitable as a dollhouse for dolls or action figures, or even large enough for you to play inside.

Before using anything from around the house to play with, be sure to get a parent's permission first. Okay, Frank Lloyd Wright, Jr.—go to it!

O N E
or more

MATERIALS

✐ Objects around the house

Nickel Golf

MATERIALS

✎ Coins (preferably a different denomination for each player)

One caveat before you start reading about Nickel Golf: The game requires two little indentations in your lawn. If you're not agreeable to that, skip this activity and choose something else for your child to do after school today. But if two tiny indentations don't bother you, read on.

One indentation, teacup-sized, is made by digging the heel of a shoe into the grass and turning it in a circle. Then there's a lag line, from which the player "tees off"—a straight line about 15 feet from the cup, made by scratching with the heel of a shoe.

The players toss their respective coins underhand, one at a time, from behind the lag line, aiming at the hole. Each gets one throw to start; then, after each player has thrown once, everyone walks to where his coin landed, picks it up, and throws again from that place. Play continues in that manner till every player has gotten his coin into the hole. The number of throws it takes a player to get his coin in the hole is his score for that hole—though, of course, every "hole" really consists of going back to the lag line, then aiming at the same hole over again. You can play nine or eighteen holes, as in standard golf, or some other number.

Nonsense Rhymes

Here's a different sort of rhyming challenge: Rhyme a word with a nonsense word, then write a poem using that rhyme. It's not as easy as it sounds, but it's fun. You might rhyme WORD with CLURD, NONSENSE with BONSENSE, or TEACHER with GREECHER. But now . . . try writing a poem using the words CLURD or BONSENSE or GREECHER! The poem doesn't have to be long—a two-liner will do fine, though a longer poem is great! You can even use more than one set of rhymes—and more than one nonsense word—in the poem.

O N E
or more

MATERIALS

None; or paper, pen or pencil

217

Nonstop Talkers

MATERIALS

✐ Watch with a
second hand or
stopwatch or
timer

Can you talk nonstop for three minutes on an assigned subject? That's the challenge in this activity for two or more people—that is, to talk for three minutes without stopping (except long enough to breathe). One player gives another a topic. (To be fair, it has to be something the "talker" knows something about. Good examples are The Seasons or My Family or Birthdays or School. It shouldn't be anything too obscure or limiting.) The "talker" has fifteen seconds to get his thoughts together. Then he has to start speaking . . . and continue for three minutes. If he can do it, he's a winner.

Now it's the other player's turn. And if there are still more players, each of them gets a turn. Choose a new topic for each player.

This isn't a game that necessarily has just one winner. Theoretically, every player could be a winner . . . if all the players succeed in talking for three minutes nonstop.

Nuts for Boating!

Miniature sailboats made from walnut shells are fun to make and a delight to own and sail. Your child can have great fun on his own, first making such a boat—or a fleet of them—then sailing it. With friends, he can launch a whole flotilla. Here's how he proceeds to make one:

Fill half a walnut shell with modeling clay, tamping it firmly in. Don't overfill, or you'll upset the boat's balance. You want to keep the center of gravity low. Insert a toothpick into the clay to use as a mast, and glue a bit of fabric to it for a sail.

The boat will actually float in a tub, sink, wading pool, pond, or puddle.

O N E
or more

MATERIALS

- Walnut shell, modeling clay, toothpick, small bit of material, glue

Occupied—and Beyond

MATERIALS

- Poster board (preferably) or cardboard, paint or crayons or colored marking pens, cup hook, glue, hole punch, scissors

Does your child sometimes want privacy? Does merely closing the door not seem to be guarantee enough? Airplane lavatories have OCCUPIED signs that bolster the message the locked door gives. Hotel rooms have DO NOT DISTURB signs to keep the maid out. And now your child's room can have its own set of signs.

The choice of message is up to your child. She might choose PLEASE KNOCK FIRST, BUSY, SSSH— SLEEPING, or COME IN. Whatever choice she decides on, she writes the message on poster board, decorates it with a design (optional), and punches a hole in the middle of the top of the sign. Then all you have to do is glue a cup hook to her door, and she can hang the appropriate sign up to let the world know whether she wants company right now or not . . . and whether that company is expected to knock before entering.

220

Odds 'n' Evens Chase

Mark the numbers 1 through 6 on each foam rubber cube. Using chalk if drawing on pavement or perhaps paint on grass, draw a center line and a finish line on either side of it. How far apart you draw the lines will depend on the ages of the players and the space available.

Divide the players into two teams, "odds" and "evens." They line up facing each other about 3 feet apart on either side of the center line. Give one player on each team a die. At a signal, both toss their dice into the middle. If the total that comes up is an odd number, the players on the "odd" team have to quickly turn around and hotfoot it to their finish line, pursued by the players from the "even" team. If the total comes up an even number, the reverse occurs.

If one of the chasers tags a runner, that runner is out of the game. If a runner crosses the finish line untagged, however, he's safe (for the moment!) and returns to his position facing the center line, ready for the cubes to be tossed again. Play continues till all the players of one team have been eliminated. The other team is the winner.

GROUP

MATERIALS

- Two fairly large foam rubber cubes (available at most crafts stores or fabric shops), marking pen, chalk or paint

221

Official Forms

MATERIALS

🖉 Any official forms you can get your hands on, from work or elsewhere, such as job applications, insurance claim forms, blank tax return forms, and even While You Were Out blanks and old checks from closed accounts

Don't you just hate filling out endless forms? So do I. So do most people. But kids, believe it or not, find them fascinating! When I was a child, I got my hands on some While You Were Outs and, believe it or not, had fun filling in bogus messages. I've known of kids of more recent vintage who actually—gasp!—enjoyed filling out insurance claim forms! (It's easier when you can make up the information according to whim, isn't it?)

Employment applications, forms to open bank accounts . . . even the dread IRS form 1040—anything is fair game. Kids are fascinated by filling in the blanks, and even you may become fascinated when you get a look at some of the answers your child gives. I'll bet you never knew your son had nine kids and bought his home for $12.98!

The activity even has a practical benefit: If your child becomes comfortable with such blanks through filling them in play, he's less likely to become flummoxed when he has to fill one out for real a few years down the road.

Once upon a Time, When I Was Invisible

The next time your child complains that he's bored because there's nothing to do, and if it turns out that he really has finished his homework, suggest he tell you a story about when he was invisible.

"But I never was invisible, Mommy!"

"But you can pretend."

He can also pretend he had X-ray vision, was 5 inches tall, was 12 feet tall, was transparent, or could melt like the Wicked Witch in *The Wizard of Oz*.

What else would you like to suggest he pretend about himself and tell stories about?

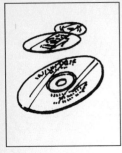

Order on the Shelves

MATERIALS

✍ Your entertainment library (CDs, audiotapes, videotapes, and even LPs if you still have some)

If the seemingly random order of your music and videotapes is actually a precise orientation known only (but known well) by you, skip this activity and go on to another one.

But if your tapes, discs, and whatnot are in no particular order, then turn your child loose on putting them to rights.

Depending on whether your music collection runs heavily to jazz, to classics, to rock, to movie sound tracks, or to a little of a lot of things, you can suggest he alphabetize by title, by performer, or by composer; you can have him break down the collection by category first; or (and this might be the most satisfying for him) you might turn him loose and ask him to devise a system.

With your videotapes, too, you may want to separate drama from comedy from musicals from kids' fare, or you may just want to lump 'em all together and alphabetize by title.

Whatever system you wind up with, he'll have the satisfaction of having done a good job, and you'll have a neat collection.

Organize Your Books

Does your child have a medium-to-large-sized collection of books? Is it in something of a jumble? Or is it in an orderly arrangement, but it's time to just organize it differently? Here are some of the ways he can organize his books. Notice that some of them can be combined (e.g., separate fiction from nonfiction and then, within each of the two categories, alphabetize by title).
• Alphabetically by title. • Alphabetically by author. • All fiction books together, all nonfiction books together, and all books of poems together. • All books on a particular subject (e.g., dinosaurs) together. • All paperbacks together and all hardbound books together.

Your child may also want to keep a list of his books—sort of like the library's card catalogue. He may want to list the title, the author, subject, and what category the book falls into (fiction, nonfiction, poetry, perhaps even plays in print—if he has any of those).

O N E

MATERIALS

✏ Your collection of books

✂ Optional: Paper, pen or pencil

Paging Geraldo!

O N E
or more

MATERIALS

✐ Camcorder

Geraldo opened Al Capone's vault. What intrepid reporter, however, dares open the door to . . . your child's room?

But seriously, folks . . . your child, assuming she's old enough to handle your camcorder responsibly, can take viewers on a guided tour of the house, perhaps pointing out the places where Significant Moments in Family History occurred. She can open the door not just to her room but also to family lore. She can interview family members.

She can figure out, on her own, the format her tape is going to take. Will it be a travelogue, an exposé, a talking heads interview, or something else again? Will she script her "program" or ad lib it? (Will the prospect of taping inside her room prompt her to—gasp!—clean the room first, or will she let the world see the mess it really is?)

Paging Geraldo . . . Junior Grade

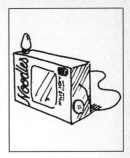

Even if your child isn't old enough to
handle a camcorder responsibly, she
can go around the house pretending to
tape-record a travelogue, interviews, an
exposé, or a documentary. With a prop in
hand—and there are lots of things that
will function well as "pretend cameras"—
she can act as a roving reporter and
imagine she's taping the shocking
conditions in her brother's room or the
gorgeous display of tulips along the
walkway.

She may actually sharpen her critical
photographer's eye or interviewer's skills
for real, even if the camera is only pretend.

O N E
or more

MATERIALS

⬤ Coffee can or
cigar box or other
"pretend camera"

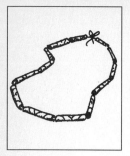

Paper Beads

Your child can make bead necklaces she and her friends can wear with enjoyment. Best of all, they're made out of recycled materials—that is, old magazines. Here's how:

Cut pennant-shaped triangles out of colorful pictures (which could even be ads) from magazines. The length of the triangle's short side should be about the same as the length of a toothpick. Place that short side of the triangle up against a toothpick and tightly roll the paper up till you reach the point at the opposite end; now apply a dab of glue to the point to hold it in place and slip the toothpick out.

Repeat the process till you have as many beads as you want. Then thread a needle with dental floss and string the beads onto the floss. The beads should cover all of the floss except the knot, and the floss's length should be sufficient that it can easily slip over the wearer's neck.

ONE
or more (each working on a separate necklace)

MATERIALS

Old magazines, scissors, glue, toothpicks, dental floss, needle

228

Paper Snowflakes

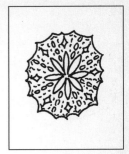

These snowflakes won't close the school, and your child can't go sledding on them, either. But they do make cheery, pretty decorations for the window of his room. Here's how he goes about making one . . . although he certainly shouldn't stop at one—he'll want to make a whole flurry of them!

Measure the long side of the paper and mark off a point 2½ inches from either the top or bottom on each side, then connect those two points and cut along that line. The result will be a square of paper 8½ by 8½ inches.

Fold the paper so that two corners diagonally across from each other meet; this will form a triangle out of the folded paper. Fold it twice more. You now have a much smaller triangle.

On each of the three sides of the folded triangle, cut several scalloped wedges. Just be sure that you leave some part of each of the three sides uncut. (You'll find you get better results from more and smaller cuts than from fewer and larger cuts.)

When you unfold the paper, hold it with one of the points facing up, not with an edge up, and you'll see that it looks like a snowflake.

O N E

MATERIALS

✐ Sheets of white typing paper, scissors, ruler, pencil

229

Party Prep

What's almost as much fun as a party? Planning for one! If your child has a birthday coming up in the next few months, draw out the fun by starting the planning and preparation early. One activity she can get into well in advance is creating party hats! Making them is even more fun than wearing them, so let your child have fun making a variety of hats for herself and her party guests.

Create a cone-shaped hat by rolling a piece of construction paper into a cone, using tape, glue, or staples to attach one side of the cone to the other. With scissors, trim the bottom of the cone so that it's even all around.

Other hats can be formed out of strips of construction paper perhaps 4 inches wide. Your child can wrap the strip around her forehead and overlap the ends, to see where she needs to glue them together. The strips can be straight or have zigzag patterns cut into them.

Decorate both cone-shaped hats and headdress-style hats with feathers, sequins, buttons, glitter, elbow macaroni, or just crayon or paint.

Anticipation is half the fun.

Patterned Snacks

Fruits and veggies are much more enticing when they're cut into shapes . . . especially the shapes your child associates with cookies. And it's fun when he cuts the shapes himself. For younger kids, you, the parent, had better do at least the slicing yourself; for really young kids, you may have to help with using the cookie cutter, too. But the resulting moons, trees, and so on will make those healthful snacks look so much more interesting to your child . . . and turn snack-time prep into a fun activity.

O N E
with parental help
in use of knife

MATERIALS

✐ Cookie cutters; slices of vegetables or fruits such as bananas, cucumbers, large radishes

Peeping at Peepers

Virtually all kids love to look at birds. Why not suggest they give them more than an "Oh—wow! Look at that!" quick glance. They can go out and deliberately look for birds, trying to spot as many different species as they can. Armed with a book identifying birds, they can look up the avian friend they've seen and find out what it is and perhaps a bit more about it, if they're interested in its habits and habitat.

Your child may even want to keep a journal, in which he records the birds he's seen and the times and places he's seen them. Birdwatching teaches not only about our feathered neighbors but also about patience and the need to be observant.

Penny Height

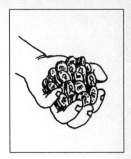

Your child lies down on the floor and stretches as far as she can while a friend, you, or anyone else, lays pennies in a straight line from her head to her toes. How many pennies tall is she? Now let her measure her friend, you, or whoever laid the pennies out for her. How many pennies tall is the other person?

T W O
or more

MATERIALS

🖎 Large quantity of pennies (and possibly nickels, dimes, and/or quarters as well)

Try the same experiment with other coins if you want. How many dimes tall is she? How many quarters or nickels tall is she? (Although pennies and dimes are close enough in size that there may not be a significant difference between her "height in pennies" and her "height in dimes," there is enough of a difference in the size of nickels and quarters that a child who is "twenty-five pennies tall" will not be "twenty-five quarters tall.")

How much does her "height in pennies/nickels/dimes/quarters" equal in actual monetary value?

233

Penny Lag

This competitive game consists simply of tossing coins underhand at a wall—indoors or out, but not on grass or carpeting—and seeing whose penny (or other coin) lands closest to the wall.

The reason for not playing on carpet or grass is so as not to eliminate the bounce factor. Throw carefully . . . gently. If you hit the wall, the coin will bounce farther away.

Players stand behind a lag line, which is created by stretching out a string. They may lean over it but not step over it. Each player tosses one coin, and the one whose coin lands closest to the wall is the winner. Then they pick up the coins and toss again.

The winner can be either the player who scored the most points in twenty (or some other number) throws or the first player to score 10 (or some other number) points.

TWO
or more

MATERIALS

✎ Two coins, length of string

234

Personalized Stationery

Does your child need more than simply encouragement to sit down and write thank-you notes, or even to reply to letters from out of town friends? Maybe he'll feel differently if he has his own personalized stationery to tempt him into writing.

ONE

MATERIALS

✐ Paper, magazine, glue, scissors, fine-line marker or regular pen

He can personalize each sheet individually; but as I offer directions here, I'm going to assume you have access to a copy machine.

All he has to do is write his name at the top of the page in black or red or dark blue ink. He can write something like JOEY KRAMER or FROM JOEY or simply JOEY. He'll probably want to decorate the note, too. What he needs to do is look through magazines for a picture that catches his fancy. It could be a horse, a person fishing, a car, a drum, or it could be an abstract design, a symbol (such as a musical note), or any other illustration that's appropriately sized and printed in dark colors that will copy well. After he cuts out the illustration and glues it to the paper he's written his name on, you photocopy the whole thing. Now he has his very own stationery.

Phone Number Words

ONE

MATERIALS

✐ Phone, paper,
pencil or pen

With the proliferation of "800 numbers" that spell words, the concept of "phone number words" isn't as unfamiliar as it once was. I have a friend whose phone number (I won't give you his area code in case any pranksters read this) is 433-4346. The first numeral in his phone number is a 4; 4 is associated with G, H, and I on the phone dial. The 3 that follows can be a D, E, or F. By trying different combinations of the letters that match the numerals of his phone number, he worked out that his phone number spells out HE DID GO.

Your child can have fun converting your phone number into words. He may even come up with a phrase or word that's especially appropriate. Is his favorite activity fishing? You've lucked out if your number is 347-4464; that converts to FISHING.

236

Pick-a-Plot

This diversion has a lot in common with Sentence Ingredients (page 292). But here, instead of building a sentence with words from a bowl, you're building a whole story with ingredients from three different bowls.

Write descriptions of at least ten characters, each on a separate slip of paper, fold each, and put them into a bowl. These might be such descriptions as a veterinarian, a mean teacher, a rabbit, a gnome, or a funny neighbor.

In another bowl, put slips of paper containing descriptions of things people might want to do, such as Wants to go to Disney World, Has to deliver a truckload of diamonds, or Always wanted to be a dentist.

In the last bowl, put slips of paper with complications written on them. A complication is anything that makes life difficult or makes accomplishing something difficult: Has the measles, Is afraid of haunted houses, Has no money.

Now draw one slip out of each of the three bowls . . . and write (or recite—it doesn't have to actually be in writing) a short story based on those three elements. If several kids are playing, each draws one slip from each of the three bowls, and each has to write a story.

ONE
or more

MATERIALS

✎ Paper, pen, scissors, three bowls or hats or other containers

237

Pictures on a Frame!

ONE

MATERIALS

Wide, shiny, colorful gift wrap ribbon; scissors; glue; cardboard; photos of your child (and her brother(s)/sister(s), if any); double-faced poster tape

Whether this winds up hanging in your own home or at Grandma's, your child will have fun making it and get double pleasure when he sees it hanging on the wall.

Cut four equal lengths of wide satin-type gift wrap ribbon, each perhaps 1½ feet long. Cut four pieces of cardboard of identical width and length as the ribbon. Glue the ribbon onto the cardboard, and glue the four pieces together so that they form a square. This square is the frame.

Apply double-faced removable poster tape to the back of the frame for mounting on the wall. Using the same tape, press smallish pictures of the child into place on the frame, rather than within it. Space the pictures out around the frame so that chunks of frame show between the pictures.

As the child grows, newer pictures can easily replace some of the pictures you started with. Just gently peel the picture from the frame. The tape should release easily.

Pillow Tag

This is your basic game of tag, except that instead of tapping—or sometimes hitting or shoving—each other, the players accomplish the tag by throwing a pillow at each other. All players are armed with pillows. One player is chosen to be the first It, and he now tries to tag the other player or one of the others if there are three or more. A tagged player—one who's been successfully smacked with a pillow—becomes It and now has to try to throw his pillow at the other(s).

The game is likely to turn into a pillow fight, but that's a fun game too!

Usually two, possibly more

MATERIALS

✐ Pillow or throw pillow or other soft object such as a blackboard eraser or similar item

Ping-Pong Pounce—Competitive Version

TWO
or more

MATERIALS

✎ Ping-Pong ball,
empty coffee can
(check for rough
or sharp edges),
length of rope,
wire hanger
(check for sharp,
pointed, exposed
ends), two chairs
or chair and
doorknob or
something else to
tie the rope to

Stretch a rope out, tying each end to something—a doorknob, a drawer handle, the back of a chair, or whatever opportunity offers itself in your house. Pull on the bottom of a wire hanger till you've stretched it into a sort of diamond shape . . . something closer to a circle than its present triangular shape. Twist the hook of the hanger a quarter turn. Now hang the hanger on the rope. The diamond-shaped "hole" in the hanger should be parallel to the rope. Place the empty coffee can about 6 inches beyond the hanger.

Players stand about a foot on the near side of the hanger. Each tries to throw the Ping-Pong ball through the hanger and into the coffee can. Players score a point if they succeed, but the ball must go through the hanger first; if it lands in the can without first passing through the hanger, there is no score.

Each player throws once, then passes the ball to the next player, continuing till each player has thrown twenty-five times. Any time a player gets a "basket," she scores a point. After all players have thrown the ball twenty-five times each, the player with the highest score wins.

Ping-Pong Pounce— Solo Version

Though Ping-Pong Pounce is great fun when played competitively, it's also plenty of fun for one child playing alone (and is good practice for later competition). The setup and basic rules are the same as for the competitive version, which precedes this.

Solo challenges:

- See how many throws it takes you to score ten points.
- See how many points you can score in twenty-five throws.
- See if you can improve on your previous personal best.

O N E

MATERIALS

Ping-Pong ball, empty coffee can (check for rough or sharp edges), length of rope, wire hanger (check for sharp, pointed, exposed ends), two chairs or chair and doorknob or something else to tie the rope to

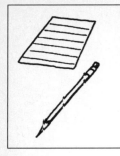

Plan to Start a Club

ONE
or more

MATERIALS

None; or paper,
pen or pencil

Though it takes at least two people to form a club, it takes only one to plan a club. Your child can have lots of fun planning to start a club, then invite his friends to join him in it. (Won't it be more convincing if he has a whole plan for the club laid out, instead of just asking his friends, "Hey, wanna start a club? I bet we could think of something to do once we get it started.")

He can start by thinking about the purpose of the club. Some examples include purely social, practice speaking a foreign language, do good deeds around neighborhood, help each other with homework, plan each other's birthday parties, put on shows or puppet shows, and trade secrets and tricks about reaching higher levels in video games.

Other things to think about include the name of the club, the club motto and/or slogan, the club password or secret sign, the location of meetings or the clubhouse, the requirements (if any) for membership, the club's activities, and the design of the club flag or pennant.

Plants of Ancient Times

Dinosaurs are extinct. So are dodo birds. Other forms of animal life have disappeared for all time, too. We all know that. But what about plant life? Are there trees, flowers, bushes, or other forms of plant life that once upon a time decorated this Earth of ours but have since gone the way of the pterodactyl?

Your child can have a fine time imagining the kinds of flowers, trees, shrubs, and such that might have existed in antediluvian times . . . and then drawing pictures of them.

His drawings may be fanciful—bushes that grow candy canes instead of flowers, for instance. Or they may be simply beautiful and thoroughly plausible—flowers of a kind not seen in recorded times that still could exist hypothetically. Or they may be very imaginative but not totally out of the realm of possibility—trees that grow in graceful curves, strikingly beautiful and unique.

Ready . . . set . . . draw!

O N E

MATERIALS

✐ Paper, crayons or fine-line markers or paints and paintbrush

Playing Office

With the proliferation of home offices, more kids than ever have a good idea of what their parents do all day. Even kids whose parents work on the outside, even kids whose parents have other-than-office-jobs, have a pretty good idea what an office is like, either from visiting one or from what they've seen on TV.

Your kids can play office too. A few supplies help—do you have any of the following you can supply them with: a nonworking (or unplugged) phone, an adding machine or calculator, a typewriter or computer, a sheaf of papers, a file folder or two, a stapler, pens, rubber bands, paper clips, rulers, message pads, old sales books, or old checkbooks from defunct accounts?

If the game seems to be wearing thin, you can always extend "office hours" by suggesting that the little entrepreneur might like to make a catalogue that shows what products she offers or that she design a bunch of the forms that are required for making a living in her new occupation.

Your child's idea of "playing office" may provide you with a very amusing insight into what he thinks you—or people in general—do at work all day.

O N E
or more (and the more, the better)

MATERIALS

✐ Any office-type equipment or supplies on hand

244

Playing to a Receptive Audience

Most kids are hams at heart. And all a ham needs is a receptive audience . . . and the teeniest bit of encouragement. Your child will get that encouragement when he comes home from school and finds his stuffed toys, action figures, or dolls lined up in a semicircle as a most receptive audience.

Your part in this, Mom, is to set the toys up in advance. Then, when your child comes home from school, tell him his audience awaits him . . . he's the star, and it's his turn to shine.

He can sing, dance, play an instrument, act out a scene, tell jokes, do magic tricks, or whatever else he may choose.

O N E
with parental preparation

MATERIALS

✐ Your child's stuffed toys or dolls or action figures

245

O N E
or more

MATERIALS

✐ Paper, pen or pencil

Pollsters, Inc.

Your child has probably heard about polls on the radio or TV. Of one hundred people surveyed, the majority said something-or-other. Four out of five people asked a question answered a certain way. People are polled on everything from whether they think the president of the country is doing a good job to what they eat for breakfast.

Does your child ever wonder what the results would be if someone took a poll at her school? She could be the one to do it. Here's how:

First compile a list of questions. They might include questions about favorites: What's your favorite song or food or book or TV show or movie or video game or boxed game? Or they might include more thoughtful questions: What's your biggest complaint about your parents? How do you think you could be a better person? What do you wish your mother would cook for dinner more often? What do you wish you could change about your dad? What's the thing you most wish your parents would stop saying?

Compile your list of questions today; then tomorrow, when you get to school, you can start taking your survey.

Popcorn Garlands

ONE

Now, here's an old-fashioned Christmas decoration your child can create as soon as she's old enough to use a needle responsibly. Popcorn garlands have graced Christmas trees since the days before the "good old days." They're a venerable tradition that's often ignored in modern times—let's bring them back. And your child can lead the way.

She starts by popping a batch of popcorn. While it's popping, she threads a darning needle with a looooooong strand of red or green thread, tying a double knot in the end. All she has to do then is pierce a kernel of popcorn with the needle and push the kernel down to the double knot, then pierce another kernel and push it down till it's up against the first one . . . and so on.

If she wants, she can intersperse cranberries with the popcorn, either at regular intervals or at irregular intervals.

When the thread is about filled up, she cuts it right at the needle, tying another double knot to hold the popcorn in place . . . and starts another strand of popcorn.

(Be sure to save a few kernels to nibble on. It wouldn't be as much fun if a few of the kernels intended for the garland didn't wind up in her stomach instead!)

MATERIALS

- Materials: Popcorn, darning needle, thimble, red and/or green thread

- Optional: Cranberries

Potato Puppets

MATERIALS

- Small potato, paring knife or apple corer, cloth or handkerchief

- Optional: Olive, carrot, pimiento, etc.; toothpicks

U sing a paring knife or an apple corer, make a hole in one end of a small potato that is just the right size to accommodate your child's finger. The potato, waggling around on her finger, is going to be a head; but a head looks pretty funny without features, so adding those is your next step. You (or your child, if she's old enough) can carve them into the spud, or you can get creative and make them out of veggies, such as a strip of pimiento for the mouth, a carrot for the nose, or two olive slices for eyes. You'll probably need toothpicks, pushed into the veggies and buried deep so that they're almost invisible, to hold the veggies in place.

A quick wrap of cloth or handkerchief around your child's hand and wrist provides clothing for the puppet; the head of the puppet moves when your child moves her finger. Long conversations can be expected.

Presenting Our Newest DJ

Do you think the DJs on radio have the coolest jobs around? You can do the same thing—for fun. You may never be broadcast on radio, but you can make a tape of your efforts and play it for your friends. And . . . who knows? It may turn out that you'll grow up to be a real DJ, and you can look back at this tape as your first "rehearsal" for the job!

One good idea is to put together a "theme tape." Choose various songs that deal with a particular topic—summertime, love, Christmas, or some other topic you choose—and introduce each one before you play it. Use a microphone (built-in or plug-in) to record your voice, then dub each taped song from the "play" deck onto the "record" deck of your twin-deck tape recorder. You want at least four songs, and if you have enough songs on your chosen theme to record a whole tape, that's even better.

The themed tape is just a suggestion, though. If you prefer, you can just record a good mix of songs that don't center around a theme.

O N E

MATERIALS

⊘ Twin-deck tape recorder with microphone, blank cassette, music already on tape

2 4 9

Preserving Grandma's Stories

Right now, your child may know some of Grandma's stories by heart, but in years to come, will he remember? What happens if Grandma moves to Arizona to retire? What happens some day when Grandma's no longer around at all?

And surely your child has other questions for Grandma: "Were there really no computer games when you were a kid? No computers at all? What did you do? No MTV either? What games did you play?"

Armed with a pen and paper or typewriter or a cassette recorder and a blank tape, your earnest reporter can ask questions and faithfully record the answers as Grandma (and Grandpa, and the other set of grandparents, if applicable) talk about their childhoods, their parents, their toys and games, how they spent their summers, and generally what life was like in those days and how life was different then from now.

At minimum, your child should type up or neatly write the transcribed results; others will want to read them too. If he wants, he can turn this into a "book" between construction paper covers.

Printed Shelf Paper

How would your child like to line his closet shelves with paper that bears his distinctive stamp . . . literally? Of course, you can buy a stamp pad and rubber stamps with such patterns as leaves, moons, or animals; but isn't it more fun when you take an even more active role? (Besides, with a homemade stamp pad, you can have pink or even turquoise ink.)

Make a stamp pad by covering the bottom of a small bowl or a cake pan with tempera paint, then lay in a folded-over paper towel or paper napkin. Or create your own paint: Mix salt, flour, and water to the consistency of thickened wall paint, adding food coloring till you have the color you want.

To make a do-it-yourself "rubber stamp," use leaves, keys, coins, or other objects found around the house or in nature. Or you can cut a sponge into whatever shape suits you. (Parental help is called for in using a knife.)

When your child gets really skilled at this art, you may even want to let him have a go at the new shelf paper you're about to put down in the kitchen.

O N E

with parental help (in the case of younger kids)

MATERIALS

Shelf paper; paper towel or paper napkin; bowl or cake pan; tempera paint or homemade paint made of salt, flour, water, food coloring; one or more of the following: leaves, keys, coins, sponge cut into an artistic shape or design

251

Probabilities— with Cards

MATERIALS

✐ A deck of cards

It's fun to pose questions of probabilities and then find the answer. A child with a mathematical or logical orientation can turn a deck of cards for hours, trying to discover how many times a certain card or sequence of cards will come up. Here are some questions your child can ask himself, then find the answer:

* How many cards will I have to turn before an Ace comes up? If I keep going, how many more cards will I have to turn before another Ace comes up?
* How many cards will I have to turn before I get three consecutive cards in a row—that is, say, a 4, a 5, and a 6 in a row with no other cards intervening?
* How many before I get four picture cards in a row with no other cards intervening?
* How many cards will I have to turn before I can turn up two Aces without seeing any picture cards?

Your child can invent his own questions and then attempt to answer them.

Probabilities—with Dice

Continuing the theme in the preceding activity, similar experiments can be done by tossing the dice from a board game. Here are some questions your child can attempt to answer:

O N E

MATERIALS

✐ Pair of dice
(many boxed
games have them)

- How many throws will it take to produce a 1 on either die?
- If she throws the dice twenty times, how many of those throws will produce a 1? How many of those throws will produce "snake eyes" (double-1)?
- If she throws the dice fifty times and keeps track of all the results, do all six numbers come up equally often? Assuming not, how often does each number come up?
- How many times will "snake eyes" come up out of twenty-five throws? Will doubling that—throwing the dice fifty times—produce exactly double that number?

Again, she can write her own probability questions, and then attempt to answer them.

Progressive Stories

T W O
or more

MATERIALS

🖉 None

The first player in this noncompetitive game starts an original story, preferably with an attention-getting beginning: "Oscar was the largest flying octopus on the planet Zork," or "When Jeff found the marble and picked it up, he had no idea he would instantly grow blue hair," or "I was surprised when I looked out my window and saw the giraffes walking past—especially when I realized all sixteen of them were green." The player can stop at the end of this first sentence or go on for a paragraph or two, but he should stop preferably at a crucial point in the story. Now the next player has to continue the story.

These stories have an odd way of changing their focus and shifting their setting so that a story that begins in the Masons' attic will frequently shift to the Brazilian jungle and then to a secret tunnel under the eerie professor's garden.

The game is over when the story comes to a logical conclusion or to an impasse, or when everyone decides it's time to play something else.

P-T Fun

From time immemorial, kids have been having fun with paper-towel tubes (P-T tubes). P-T tubes (as well as toilet paper tubes, or T-P tubes) can mean so many things for the child with a vivid imagination . . . and their appeal covers a broad age range, too.

What are some of the things a P-T tube can be?

- A pirate's telescope
- A baton
- A periscope
- An elephant's trunk

When your child tires of being a pirate, a baton major(ette), a submariner, and an elephant, what other uses can he think of for the P-T tube?

O N E

MATERIALS

- Empty paper-towel tube

Publish a Neighborhood Newsletter

MATERIALS

✐ Paper, pen or typewriter or computer (access to a photocopier if you're using a typewriter rather than a computer)

Your child can publish a newsletter even though your family's name isn't Hearst. All he has to do is gather news, type it up in article form, make duplicate copies, and distribute it.

First step: Get out in the neighborhood. Talk to the other kids (and the adults, too, if you want). Get the latest news. Did Jenny just get a new dog? Did Joey's family cat have kittens? Did Brian get all As on his report card? Did someone earn a Scouting merit badge? Did an adult on the block get a new job, get a new car, get married? It's all worth reporting in the Elm Street News.

Ask the details and write them down, then go home and type up all the news in the form of articles. And if you don't know how to make columns, you can just type across the whole page, except for margins at either side. It's the news that counts.

If you have a computer, run out a dozen copies of the newsletter (with parental permission); if not, get photocopies made.

256

Puppet Theater—1

There are many ways to make puppets. One of the easiest is to cut fairly large, fairly uniformly sized pictures out of a magazine, glue the pictures to cardboard, and cut around the pictured faces and bodies so that no cardboard or background is showing. Then glue a Popsicle stick or large, sturdy twig to the back of the cardboard, extending below the cutout figure.

Your puppet theater is a bridge table with a sheet draped over the front. Keep yourself out of sight behind the table, raising the Popsicle sticks so that the puppets appear just above the table's surface. Though you can work only two puppets at a time, you can trade one puppet for another, bringing one "offstage" (under the table) and another "onstage" right away. If there is more than one puppeteer, more puppets can be onstage simultaneously.

Of course, you'll eventually want to put on shows for an audience. But first you'll want to rehearse on your own till you've gotten comfortable at manipulating the puppets and using different voices to help your audience tell which puppet is supposed to be talking.

ONE
or more

MATERIALS

Bridge table, sheet, cardboard, glue, scissors, Popsicle sticks or sturdy large twigs, magazines

Puppet Theater—2

ONE
or more

MATERIALS

Socks, buttons, yarn, paint or felt; or paper bag, paint, yarn

In addition to making puppets in the manner suggested in the preceding activity, you can also sew buttons to a pale-colored sock as eyes and nose. Draw a mouth with paint. Felt features can be sewn on, if you prefer. And yarn makes good hair. Put the sock on your hand and work the puppet that way.

You can also paint a face on a small paper bag and glue yarn to the top for hair, then place that over your hand. (Also see Thread-Spool Puppets, page 320.)

You can act out well-known stories, write your own puppet plays, or just have two puppets improvise a conversation with each other.

Questions

Want to lose this game quickly? Answer a question with a direct answer. In the game of Questions, every question must be answered only by another question.

Let's listen to Matt and Jessica playing. Jessica: "What was the school lunch today?" If Matt's response is "Tuna salad" or "Why do birds fly?" he's out. Possible answers include: "What do you call that grey stuff with gravy?" and "When's pizza day?"

Jessica: "Is it August 15th?" Matt: "Is there school in August?" Jessica: "Don't you think school's in session too long?" Matt: "Wouldn't you rather be playing baseball?" Jessica: "Who's your favorite team?" Matt: "What's that new baseball team from Florida?" Jessica: "You mean the Marlins?" Matt: "Didn't they win the World Series?" Jessica: "I saw that last game!" She loses.

Players may not hesitate more than a second or two before speaking. They may not use a question that's already been used in this round.

With more than two players, go around in a circle. The last player left wins the round.

T W O
or more

MATERIALS

🖉 None

259

Quick-Think Categories

T W O
or more

MATERIALS

✐ Paper, pens or pencils, stopwatch or timer or egg timer or regular watch (if none of the preceding items is available)

✂ Optional: Unabridged dictionary (for settling disputes)

Each game consists of as many rounds as there are players. The first player calls out a category—say, Kinds of Flowers or Colleges or Native American Tribes. One player starts the stopwatch or egg timer, and everyone starts writing as many examples of things in that category as each can think of. If you're using a stopwatch, your time is two minutes. Egg timers are usually set for three minutes. If you're not using a timer that dings, don't worry if the time goes a little over before anyone notices. Everyone will have had the same advantage.

When the time is up, everyone reads his list. Any item that has been thought of by more than one player gets crossed off each list. Players score one point for each item they alone thought of. When each player has had a chance to choose a category, the game is over. The player with the most points wins.

There are no penalties for misspelling. And in case someone challenges, "I never heard of that plant," an unabridged dictionary is a good thing to have on hand.

Ramp Bowling

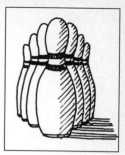

This game is basically like any other bowling game—objects are set up in order to be knocked down—but with a twist: The ball is launched not by being propelled by the hand but by being rolled down an incline. There's a lot more of the element of chance here. And there's plenty of fun.

Getting the angle of incline right is tricky—too fast, and the ball is more likely to roll off the sides of the ramp; too slow, and you won't get enough speed to knock down many pins. You probably want the raised end around a foot or two off the ground.

Players release the ball at the top of the ramp and hope it goes straight and knocks lots of pins over. Players can play and score according to regulation bowling rules or according to the rules for T-P Bowling (page 330).

ONE
or more

MATERIALS

✐ A 2- to 4-foot length of 1-inch lumber, something to prop one end of it up on, bowling pins from a toy bowling set or such makeshift pins as washed-out empty milk cartons or tall plastic drinking cups or empty pill bottles, a ball of a suitable size to aim at your "pins"

O N E

MATERIALS

Magazines,
scissors, glue,
typing paper or
construction
paper

"Ransom" Stories

These stories take their name from the way they're put together—in the manner of the classic ransom note, in which words are clipped from a magazine or newspaper and glued down on a page. I'm not suggesting you use newspaper, only because of the ink-smear factor, though you certainly can if you want, or if your household is deficient in magazines.

The idea is for your child to clip out one word at a time from anywhere in a magazine—stories, ads, photo captions—gluing each word down on a sheet (or several sheets) of paper to create a story that makes some sense.

Quite a bit of creativity is involved in looking over pages and pages of words to select words that in combination with each other will create a cohesive, reasonably interesting story. How well will your child do at it? What sort of story will he "write"?

The Real Story of . . .

Of course it's fun to tell a story to others and not just make it up for yourself. But before you tell it to others, you may want to work it out in your own head or even write the story down on paper.

The idea here is to write your own version of a famous story—the supposedly real story of Robin Hood, of Cinderella, or even of a famous historical event, like Washington crossing the Delaware or Betsy Ross sewing the first flag.

If you come up with a really good story, you may even want to turn it into a homemade book. Create a front and back cover with construction paper, using crayons or paint to write your title and your name (very important—you're the author!) and perhaps draw an illustration as well. Staple the typed or hand-printed story inside.

O N E
or more

MATERIALS

✏ None; or paper, pen or pencil

✂ Optional: Construction paper, crayons or paints, stapler

Red Light, Green Light

GROUP
(and the larger, the better)

MATERIALS

✐ None

This game is similar to "Mother, May I?" (page 203). Once again, you have one player standing on an imaginary line (this time she is known as It, rather than Mother) and the rest of the players in a straight line some distance away, each trying to be the first to cross the finish line and win. But in Red Light, Green Light, all the players move together on the commands of It.

The commands are "Red light" and "Green light." It turns her back to the players and yells "Green light!" At this signal, the players then hurry toward the finish line. But as soon as It yells "Red light!" and spins around to face the other players, they all must freeze. Anyone It catches moving is sent back to the starting line.

It's hard to stop fast at a dead run. It may call "Red Light!" a split second after calling "Green Light!" The idea is to advance at the fastest speed at which you can still freeze instantly at the command.

The first player to successfully cross the finish line wins and becomes It for the next game.

264

Red Rover— Version 1

Two lines mark the playing field in Red Rover, and players may want to use chalk to draw those two lines (assuming they're playing on pavement and not grass). But the old reliable imaginary line is fine too—so are two opposing curbs, if your street is free enough of traffic for safe play.

Choose a player to be It. It stands in the space between the two lines while all the other players line up behind one of the lines. Now It chants, "Red Rover, Red Rover, let Marsha come over." Marsha tries to run from the one line to the other without It tagging her. She can sprint, zigzag, or take any other action she wants, as long as she stays within the defined playing area. If It tags her before she reaches the boundary, she becomes It. If Marsha makes it across safely, It now calls out another player: "Red Rover, Red Rover, let Vic cross over."

When a player is caught and becomes It for a new game, all the players return to waiting behind one line for the new It to call them.

G R O U P

MATERIALS

- None (except possibly chalk to draw lines)

265

Red Rover—
Version 2

MATERIALS

✐ None (except possibly chalk to draw lines)

This version is played according to all the rules of the version preceding this, with one notable exception. In the first version, it's too easy for It to stand in front of the player he's calling over, which makes it difficult for that player to outrun It and get to the other side safely. It can be done, but the odds are long against the runner. This side evens up that inequity.

In this version, a category is chosen at the start of the game—for instance, Baseball Teams. Every player decides on a team without telling anyone what team he's chosen. When It calls out, "Red Rover, Red Rover, let the Mets come over," every player who has chosen the Mets must run.

Since It has no idea who's going to respond to the call, he can't position himself directly in front of the player he's about to call. In fact, it may be that no one has decided they're the Mets, or maybe three players will rush headlong across the space. After a few rounds of this, the players redefine themselves so that It doesn't have all the players pegged.

A Report Card for Your Teacher

O N E

MATERIALS

Typing paper or construction paper

Four times a year, your child's teacher gets to pass judgment on him. Does he read well? Know his history? Try hard? Four times a year, the teacher sends home the dreaded report card.

But what if the tables were turned? What if students got to grade their teachers? How would your child's teacher fare if your kid were the one doing the grading?

Your child can write a report card that grades his teacher on the items he thinks are most important. What would some of them be? Start with these:

- GRADES FAIRLY
- AVOIDS PLAYING FAVORITES
- EXPLAINS SCHOOLWORK CLEARLY
- HAS REASONABLE EXPECTATIONS

What would your child add to that? And how would he grade his teacher? (If his teacher has a good sense of humor and your child is honest and fair in his grading, maybe he can even give the teacher the report card!)

267

Reverse Silhouette

By shining a strong light on a person, you can cast their shadow on a piece of paper. And by moving the light nearer to or farther from the subject, you can make that shadow get larger or smaller. If your child lines up you, one of his friends, or anyone else in such a manner, he can contrive to have the silhouette fill almost all the white paper, drawing around the silhouette with a pencil.

The subject can now be excused to go do something more fun than standing still. Meanwhile, your child cuts along the pencil line, till the silhouette has been cut away from the rest of the paper. After applying glue to the side he drew on, he pastes it down on the black construction paper. The result is a reverse silhouette— white on black instead of vice versa—that he can give as a gift to the person who sat for the "portrait."

ONE
plus the subject of
the silhouette

MATERIALS

Strong light, two large sheets of paper (one white, one black), glue, scissors

268

Rhythm Sticks

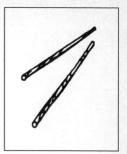

Junior musicians who lack instruments can have the feeling of making music if they tap two sticks together in time to recorded music. It may not be melodic, but percussion is part of music too. And while drums are the best-known percussion instrument, your child, if he lacks a drum or makeshift, can still keep the beat with rhythm sticks.

Put a piece of familiar music on the stereo and tell your child to listen. He can hit the sticks together on every downbeat or, if he's a little older and more musically sophisticated, hit on the offbeat.

Another rhythmic possibility is to use the two sticks in the manner of drumsticks, hitting on the phone book. Regular books should not be abused as pseudo-drums, but no one (except possibly the phone company) is going to take offense at the phone book being "mistreated."

O N E

MATERIALS

✐ Two fairly solid sticks (such as dowels), recorded music

Riddle Squares

TWO
or more

MATERIALS

✐ Chalk, rocks or stones

On the sidewalk (or on the street in a traffic-safe cul de sac), use chalk to draw a series of ten large squares laid out in an oblong, as in the game of hopscotch. Draw a lag line about a foot back of the nearest square.

The first player stands behind the lag line, throws the rock, and tries to land it in any square. If he succeeds in getting it totally within the lines of that square, he asks a riddle of any other player of his choice. If the other player answers the riddle correctly, the other player writes his initials in the square; if he fails, the asking player writes his initials in the square. Either way, it is now the next player's turn to throw the rock. If the first player fails to land the rock completely within a square, it becomes the next player's turn right away.

No other player may now claim that square. If another player lands his rock within that square, it's as if he'd failed to get his rock within a square, as that square is already taken. Play continues in this manner until all the squares are claimed. At that point, the player who "owns" the most squares is the winner.

Ring Toss—
Horseshoe Rules

Each player needs two rings; make them by tying into a circle the heaviest rope you can find. (Hemp is better than cotton.) A length of rope between 16 and 20 inches should yield a ring about 5 inches in diameter. If the ring doesn't remain horizontal when held horizontally in one hand, it's not heavy or stiff enough. To distinguish players' rings, apply a splotch of paint or nailpolish to one pair.

You can play with one target stick, tossing all four rings at that stick from behind a string you've laid out, then retrieving them and tossing again. Bury target sticks partway in the ground to anchor them; they should stick up from the ground at least 6 inches. Tossing distance will depend on the players' age and proficiency.

Scoring: A ring goes over the stake and stays there—3 points; a ring leans against the stake—2 points; a ring lands within one ring's width of the stake—1 point. The game ends when one player scores at least 21 points and is ahead by 2 points.

T W O

MATERIALS

✐ Four rings made from 16- to 20-inch lengths of heavy rope, one or two stakes or sticks or dowels or similar item, paint or nailpolish or tape

Ring Toss—Quoits Rules

TWO

MATERIALS

✐ Four rings made from 16- to 20-inch lengths of heavy rope, one or two stakes or sticks or dowels or similar item, paint or nailpolish or tape

Follow the rules for Ring Toss on the previous page, except for scoring. Under quoits rules, the player with the ring closest to the stake receives 1 point for each ring that lands closer to the stake than the other player's ring(s) and 3 points for a ringer.

The game is over when one player scores 21 points and is ahead by 2 points. (If someone reaches 21 but isn't ahead by 2 points, play continues till someone is ahead by 2 points.)

Robinson Radio Theatre

Robinson is hypothetically your last
name; substitute your real last name
before the first of this series of
homegrown radio dramas (or comedies)
is "broadcast." The "radio" in this case is
a cassette recorder. And the actor is (or
actors are) your child (or children).

Your kids can write "radio plays" and
perform them into the mike of a cassette
recorder, then push "play" when the whole
family's gathered together and have the
pleasure of hearing themselves as "radio
actors" along with the rest of the family.
Have only one child? No problem—by
changing his voice for the different
characters, he can assume all the parts in
the drama . . . providing he writes a two-
or three-character show.

Or, if your child is an "only" and
wants a larger cast of characters, he can
write the script on his own, then get his
friends over to help him record it on
another occasion.

Now let's see . . . they give Oscars for
movies, Emmys for TV, Tonys for
Broadway, and Grammys for records.
What do they give for mock radio?

O N E
or more

MATERIALS

✐ Paper, pen or
pencil, cassette
player and blank
tape

Rock, Scissors, Paper

MATERIALS

✐ None

Also known to some as Scissors, Paper, Stone, this is both played as a game unto itself and used as a method of choosing who goes first in some other game.

The mechanics are very simple: You and your opponent each put one hand behind your back and do one of three things with it: curl it in a fist (representing a rock or stone), stretch it out flat (representing a sheet of paper), or curl up your third and fourth fingers while holding your index and middle finger in a V (representing a pair of scissors). Together, count aloud: "One, two, three." On "three," you each quickly bring your hand out front, showing which configuration your hand is in.

The results follow real life, which makes them easy to remember: Rock dulls scissors. Scissors cut paper. Paper wraps rock. In other words, if one player shows a "rock" hand and the other shows "paper," the player showing "paper" wins. And so forth. If both players show the same configuration, it's a tie and a do-over.

Rockin' Santa

Santa's going to rock on! That's because Santa is a rock—a smooth, flat rock that your child is going to decorate with a face to look like the Jolly Old Elf. Here's how:

Wash the rock and let it dry. When it's totally dry, paint eyes, a nose, and red cheeks on it. Skip the mouth—it would be hidden by the mustache and beard. And that mustache and beard are what you're going to create next, tearing or cutting suitable-sized pieces of cotton and gluing them in place. If you want, you can give old Santa a few wisps of white hair, too.

Cut a cap for Santa out of red construction paper . . . a drooping cone shape, to the tip of which you can glue more white cotton. Paste the hat to the top of the surface of the rock. (In other words, the rock face doesn't literally go into the hat.)

This Santa doesn't have to visit once a year. He can be a permanent guest.

O N E

MATERIALS

- A smooth, flat rock that's fairly round or oval, as opposed to asymmetrical; white cotton; red felt; glue; paint; scissors

Roving Reporter

MATERIALS

⬦ Cassette recorder,
blank tape

"This is your roving reporter, Johnny Armstrong, on Elm Street, talking to the kids on the street. Today's question is, 'Should school be in session six days a week but let out earlier in the day?' What do you think? And your name is . . ."

"This is Lisa Lawrence, your girl-on-the-street, asking questions of kids just like you. Today's question is, 'What do you think is a fair punishment when time-outs don't work? Should parents spank their kids?' Here's a kid who looks like he has something to say. What's your name?"

With a cassette recorder in hand, your child can go up and down the street after school, talking to the kids who are out playing or ringing doorbells to talk to kids who are inside. Questions about school, family life, discipline, homework, toys and games, sports, and television are generally pretty good for eliciting opinions from other kids.

Be sure to thank each interviewee for his or her opinion, and identify yourself once again in your sign-off. Then "broadcast the show" by playing the tape back for all the kids who participated . . . and anyone else who wants to listen.

Rubber Band Knockdown

Each player leans two playing cards against each other, on their short ends, in such a way that they support each other and both stand up. All players stand back about three feet from their cards, take aim with their rubber bands, and try to hit their own pair of cards with their rubber bands. Each player tries to hit his cards accurately enough that he knocks his pair of cards down. If he's the first to do so, he's the winner. If he knocks another player's cards down, that player is declared winner.

T W O
or more

MATERIALS

✐ Two playing cards and a rubber band per player

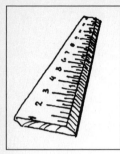

Ruler Challenge

MATERIALS

✎ 12-inch ruler, tennis ball or rubber ball or jacks ball

How steady are your hands? How quick are your reactions? Can you hold one end of a ruler, place a ball next to your hand, grab the other end of the ruler, tilt it just a little so that the ball starts to slide down toward the other end of the ruler, and hold the ruler steadily enough that the ball rolls from one end to the other without falling off?

That's what your child is asked to do in this challenge. Does it sound easy? Well, the instructions are simple enough, but carrying it out is anything but. Obviously, if your ruler is sloped on one side, you want to use the other side, the flat side, for this game.

Do you like a tough challenge? Good, because you've got one here.

Run, Sheep, Run

Establish boundaries and choose who'll be It and who'll be Shepherd. Everyone else is a sheep.

The sheep and Shepherd secretly choose verbal signals (perhaps numbers, words, or animal sounds) indicating that It is near them, is out of sight, is looking the other way, or any other clue they feel is useful.

It hides her eyes and counts to 100; the sheep and Shepherd find one hiding place for all the sheep. The Shepherd returns to Home Base before It reaches 100. It goes looking for the sheep; the Shepherd accompanies her and calls out signals to the hidden sheep. Some will be meaningless, intended to confuse It.

When the Shepherd decides it's safe, she calls, "Run, Sheep, Run!" and the sheep pelt toward Home Base. Hearing the call, It races back to Home Base too, trying to arrive before the sheep; failing that, she tries to tag the slower members of the flock.

If It doesn't tag any sheep, the game is over, and she's stuck being It for the new game. If It does tag sheep, the first one she tags is the new It. If It gets back to Home Base ahead of any sheep, she decides who is It for the next game.

GROUP

MATERIALS

✎ None

279

Sand Jars

MATERIALS

Sand, food coloring, water, newspaper, one jar or deep bowl for each color you are creating, a stick or a utensil for mixing the sand, one glass or clear plastic jar with a lid for the finished product

In a bowl or jar, mix a little water and some food coloring. The more coloring you use, the more intense will be the color of the sand. To get a color not among the four basics, mix two colors—for example red and blue to get purple (add more water for a lighter lilac). Now add some sand. Don't use too much colored water; you don't want the sand to get flooded, just saturated enough to absorb the color uniformly. Stir it with a stick or fork or spoon. Dump the sand on a piece of newspaper and spread it out to dry.

Repeat the process using a different color, spreading that sand out on a different sheet of newspaper, and continue till you have as many different colors as you want.

When the sand is dry, carefully dump one layer of sand (perhaps between ¼ inch and 1 inch thick) into the clean, dry jar. Now add a layer of a different color. Continue varying the layers—you can use any of the colors several times each—till the jar is packed full. And do pack it tightly, to guard against shifting. Put the lid on.

The layers don't have to be exactly level—a slope adds visual interest.

Sardines

In this reverse on Hide 'n' Seek, it's It who hides, while everyone else has to find him. After agreeing on boundaries, everyone except It counts to 100, while It hides. Then—each going his separate way—everyone goes looking for It. The first person to find him doesn't call out or tag It; he simply squeezes in with It and waits to be found by the next person . . . who, similarly, squeezes in with the others and waits for more finders.

GROUP
(and the larger, the better)

MATERIALS

✐ None

As more and more people find It and all the other hiders, it grows harder and harder to hide. First of all, the group of hiders is getting pretty darn bulky by now; additionally, most groups have trouble suppressing giggles. One by one, the seekers find the ever-larger group of hiders.

Eventually one person is left who hasn't found the group of hiders. That last person is declared It, and the game starts all over with this new It hiding while everyone else counts to 100.

Sawtooth Trees

MATERIALS

- Whatever trees and bushes are in your yard or neighborhood

A child may have trouble remembering the names of different trees or bushes, but he can usually remember any distinguishing characteristic of one leaf or another. I remembered maples as pointy-leaf trees before I knew their proper names, just as I knew the "orange light parkway" by that sobriquet long before I knew it was the Cross-Island Parkway.

How many distinguishing names can your child invent for the various greenery around your yard or your neighborhood?

Score-a-Goal

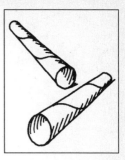

Here's yet another game that can be played as either a solo challenge or competitively. The setup: Place two P-T tubes (don't use T-P tubes—they're not long enough) parallel to each other and 2 inches apart on the floor indoors or the ground outdoors. If playing indoors, stretch a string perpendicular to the tubes, a foot away from the nearer end of them. If playing outdoors on grass or dirt, use string also; on pavement, mark a chalk line.

Player stands behind the lag line and rolls a coin or checker, attempting to roll it between the two P-T tubes so that it continues beyond them and rolls out at the other end. If it does, she scores a point. If it fails to go between the tubes or fails to make it through at the other end, there is no score.

This is fun to play "just for fun," as well as competitively to see who can score the most points in ten or twenty-five rolls.

O N E
or more

MATERIALS

✐ Checker or coin, two paper towel tubes, piece of string or chalk

ONE

MATERIALS

✐ Paper, pen or pencil

Score-a-Name

Though this is a competition of sorts, only one player is needed. You see, it's not a competition between players, but rather between names. This competition is definitely for kids who like numbers. First write all the letters of the alphabet on a piece of paper. Now assign number values to each, by writing the number 1 below A, number 2 below B, 3 below C, and so on.

If your name is Betsy, you would add up the value of the letters in your name (2 for B, 5 for E, 20 for T, 19 for S, and 24 for Y, for a total of 70). Is your sister's name Kim? What are the letter values of K, I, and M? Is your friend's name Ashleigh? What are the letter values of that name? Who has the winning name?

What if you use the long form of each of your names (Elizabeth instead of Betsy, even though you're always called Betsy, Kimberly instead of Kim, and so on)? Does that change the results?

Scrambled Words

You know how to play scrambled words—someone shows you a list of words whose letters have been scrambled, or prints them in the newspaper or a puzzle book, and you have to rearrange the letters to find the original words (e.g., PEHES is SHEEP, AORR is ROAR, LUIBD is BUILD, and LUBL is BULL).

Your child can play too, although you'll want to keep the words simple, especially if your child only learned to read last year. (Naturally, if she's a sixth-grader or reads at eighth-grade level, the words can be longer and the scrambles more confounding.)

For one child playing alone, offer her a list of scrambled words to rearrange into proper words. For two or more kids playing competitively, offer them identical lists, and see who can de-scramble her list first. For two or more kids playing cooperatively, give them a long list and let them all work on all the words together. Finally, for two or more kids without parental help, let them each construct a list, all the lists to be composed of the same number of words, with a letter limit on words (probably nothing longer than five letters), and then trade lists with each other, each trying to solve the other's scrambles.

O N E
or more, with parental preparation

MATERIALS

✐ Paper, pen or pencil

285

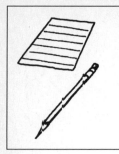

Scrambled Words Plus

O N E
or more, with parental preparation

MATERIALS

✐ Paper, pen or pencil

A variation on the preceding game, this game presents a real word and requires that your child not only rearrange the letters but also add a letter to them, to come up with a different real word. Note that it is not enough to merely add a letter (add B to OIL and get BOIL, add I to PLAN and get PLAIN)—the letters must be rearranged. This game may be played in all the various forms—one child or more, competitive or not—that apply to the preceding game.

Here are some examples to get you started: The first word shown is the word you'd give your child. The second word is one possible correct answer he could come up with. Note that other answers may be equally right. NAIL to PLAIN, SAID to ASIDE, MAIL to CLAIM, REAL to ALTER, PLEA to APPLE, CHAR to REACH, MILE to SLIME, SLAM to MAILS, ARTS to SMART, TENOR to ROTTEN.

Scratch Paintings

Paint various colors in a random design across the page. You can fill large areas with different colors, paint in great swoops, or work it however you like, but the idea is for the arrangement of colors to be random.

When the paint is quite dry, cover the whole thing with a thick application of black crayon. Cover the entire palette of colors, till you have a picture of midnight when it's moonless and starless.

Now take the coin and begin to scratch off the crayon. You can scratch in random swoops and swirls, or you can draw an actual picture if you prefer. The random method tends to produce more satisfying pictures, but do whichever suits you best. As you scratch the crayon off the paint below, splotches and streaks of colors will appear, peeking through the black crayon.

Finished scratching? Then your picture's finished too!

O N E

MATERIALS

✐ Paper, paint in various colors and paintbrush, black crayon, coin

287

Annie's Clearance Sale

Sears, Roebuck, and Annie

O N E

MATERIALS

- Items your child is ready to get rid of, paper, pen or pencil or typewriter

- Optional but helpful: Access to a photocopier

What does your child do with her cast-off toys? Is she notably reluctant to part with toys she never plays with anymore, dolls that haven't been out of the toy chest in years, and comic books she's read so often she knows the dialogue by heart?

An end to your struggle is at hand. What child can resist the lure of cold, hard cash? All she has to do is write, neatly and with as appealing descriptions as she's capable of, a "catalogue" of her castoffs . . . including reasonable prices for which she'd be willing to part with each item.

If she creates this on a computer, she can run off multiple copies and pass them around to her friends. If she types her catalogue or handwrites it, she'll need access to a photocopier in order to make multiple copies.

You may want to require that she clear every item with you before listing it. Some kids who refuse to relinquish a single toy to the giveaway pile have been known to offer up heirlooms when the prospect of payment rears its head.

288

Seed Mosaics

First get your materials ready—separate the various types of seeds, and put each type into a separate bowl or into muffin tins or egg cartons, which offer different compartments for the different types of seeds.

Now draw the picture—possibly but not necessarily abstract—that you want to fill in with the seeds. Use pencil and press lightly. Erase and redraw as needed. Remember that you want areas that you can fill in, not straight lines.

Spread one area of the picture at a time with glue, sprinkling seeds (or beans or whatever) over the glue till the seeds cover the glue completely. Shake the cardboard to dislodge excess seeds and get them off the picture. Then fill in the next area to be covered with the same type of seed.

When you're finished with all the areas to be covered in, say, sesame seeds, start gluing the spots to be covered in, say, caraway seeds. Continue till you've covered all the areas on the picture that are to be filled in. Let it dry completely, and hang it . . . or present it as a gift to Grandma.

O N E
or more (each working on a separate picture)

MATERIALS

✐ Cardboard; glue; pencil; muffin tin or egg carton or bowls; seeds and similar items such as beans, lentils, rice, sunflower seeds, popcorn kernels, split peas

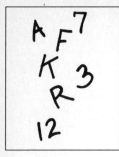

Send a Coded Message—1

TWO
or more

MATERIALS

✐ Four pieces of paper, pencil or pen

You can send secret messages back and forth with a friend with a secret code key. Write all the letters from A to Z on a sheet of paper. Now write all the letters again, underneath the first letters, but in a different order.

The easiest way is a one-step substitution: Under A write B, under B write C, and so on. Much more difficult is a random substitution: Write the letters under the first set in no particular order, making sure you have used each letter once and only once.

On another piece of paper, write a secret message to send to a friend. Now encode it, using the key you have written out. Does it say MRS. WEBER AND HER DOG LOOK LIKE EACH OTHER? Look on your key for the letter to substitute for M, and write that letter below the M, and so on. Continue till you have the whole message encoded. Now copy just the coded message on another piece of paper. Give that message to your friend with the code key so that he can decipher it and send another coded message back to you.

290

Send a Coded Message—2

T W O
or more

MATERIALS

✎ Two copies of the Morse Code (reproduced below) (one for you and one for a friend), pencil with eraser, paper

Though you need someone else to send these coded messages to, she doesn't have to be with you when you write the message. You can encode a message, then give it to a friend the next time you see her, along with a copy of the Morse Code so that she can read your message and write one back to you for you to decode and read.

In the Morse Code, each letter is represented by one or more dots and dashes. Separate each letter from the next by enough space that your friend can tell where one letter ends and the next begins. For example, write Hi this way: . . . . . .

Here's the key:

A . —	N — .
B — . . .	O — — —
C — . — .	P . — — .
D — . .	Q — — . —
E .	R . — .
F . . — .	S . . .
G — — .	T —
H	U . . —
I . .	V . . . —
J . — — —	W . — —
K — . —	X — . . —
L . — . .	Y — . — —
M — —	Z — — . .

291

Sentence Ingredients

ONE
or more

MATERIALS

Paper, pen or
pencil, scissors,
bowl or hat or
other container

Here's another activity that's fun for one and lots more silly (and noncompetitive) fun for more than one. Write an assortment of words on paper. You probably want at least twenty words for solo play, something more for multiplayer games. Mix your parts of speech, including some nouns, some verbs, some adjectives, and some adverbs. Leave space around each word so that you can cut each word out and fold it up. Drop the folded words into a bowl or similar container.

Select four words out of the bowl at random and create one sentence that utilizes all four words. It's okay to use another form of the same word (for instance HORSES if the word is HORSE, RAN if the word is RUN). If the four words are GREEN, PONY, SKIP, and HOUSE, the sentence might be, John came out of the HOUSE and SKIPPED with surprise when he saw the GREEN PONY in the yard.

Kids often tend to try for silly sentences, but this game will likely evolve into a fit of the giggles even without a deliberate attempt at silliness.

Shared Birthdays

Do you share a birthday with a famous person? The almanac can tell you. Look up your birthday in the almanac, and see who your "birthday twin" is. Then look up that person's biography in an encyclopedia (or on the Internet).

If you'd like, use that person and some aspect of his life as a theme for your next birthday party. You could even have a party in the style of parties as they were given in his time.

ONE
or more

MATERIALS

Almanac, encyclopedia (or computer with Internet access)

Sheet Ball

MATERIALS

✐ Old sheet,
scissors, tennis
ball or rubber
ball, clothesline
or rope,
clothespins

Like so many other competitive games (for instance, basketball), this one's also fun to play alone, trying to score as many points as you can, trying to better your previous best score, trying to improve your skills, or trying tricks (like scoring with your eyes closed).

Cut a hole perhaps 5 inches across in the sheet, and hang the sheet from the clothesline. How far back your child should stand will depend on her age; what's a fair distance for a nine-year-old is too easy for an eleven-year-old and too difficult for a child of six. If she's getting the ball into the hole every time, she's standing too far forward; if she never scores, she's too far back (or this just isn't her game).

The game is simplicity itself: Stand at the designated spot . . . throw . . . and try to score by getting the ball through the hole. Two kids playing together can compete, but one child can have a fine time playing Sheet Ball by herself.

Shooting Stars

There are some phrases that have one meaning but sound like they might mean something else. An example of this is "shooting stars." Shooting stars are actually meteors that streak across the sky. Now think about the expression "shooting stars" and let your mind wander. Did you start thinking of a star in the sky drawing a water pistol and shooting another star?

What other such expressions can you think of? Draw funny pictures to illustrate these expressions the way they might be interpreted.

O N E
or more

MATERIALS

Paper, crayons

ONE
or more

MATERIALS

✐ None

The Silver Rule

Many people agree that the Golden Rule is one of the most important rules for getting along with others in this world. Most of the major religions have this rule, expressed in one set of words or another. Most commonly, it's phrased like this: "Do unto others as you'd have them do unto you." To some people, this rule is phrased like this: "What is hateful to thee, do not unto others." Still others express it in different words. But almost everyone agrees on its importance.

What's another good, important rule to remember? If "Do unto others . . ." is the most important, what's the second-most important, at least in your opinion? You could call it the Silver Rule.

If you'd like, once you've decided on your Silver Rule, you can go on and think of still other important rules for successful, peaceful living.

Snail

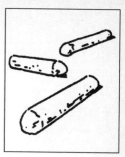

Use chalk to draw a series of contiguous boxes on the pavement. The number of boxes is up to you—the more boxes, the more difficult the game—but each box should be slightly larger than a player's foot. The traditional shape for the sequence of boxes is snail-like, winding around, but if your playing field is narrow, you can draw them in a straight line.

Players must hop from the first square to the last without changing feet, setting the other foot down, stepping on any lines, or hopping out of the snail. A player who succeeds gets to claim a square for herself by writing her initials in it. After she's tried, whether she succeeds or not, it's now the other player's turn.

Once a player has claimed a square, she is free to put both feet down in it while hopping through the snail on future turns. On the other hand, the other player may not hop into it at all but must hop over it. It's to a player's advantage to claim several squares in a row; this would require the other player to hop across all of them as she progresses through the snail—a perhaps impossible task.

When one player is so stymied that navigating the snail is impossible for her, the other player is declared the winner.

T W O

MATERIALS

✐ Chalk

ONE

MATERIALS

- Jar with screw-on lid, pinecone less tall than the jar is deep, glue, baby oil, silver glitter, newspaper to work over

Snow Jar

You've seen snow globes, those fascinating glass balls with snowscapes inside. Shake the globe or turn it upside down, then set it to rest right-side up, and watch the "snow fall."

Your child can have not only the pleasure of owning one of these but also the fun of making it herself. Here's how:

Glue a pinecone to the middle of the lid of a jar and allow it to dry completely. Fill the jar almost completely with baby oil and add a handful of silver glitter. Screw the lid onto the jar very tightly. Turn the jar upside down and shake. Watch the "snow" fall on the "tree."

Solitaire Golf

Place seven cards across in a row, then lay seven more on top of those, continuing till you have five layers. Place cards so that you can see each one. The remaining seventeen cards form a draw stack.

O N E
or more

MATERIALS

✑ A deck of cards (or a deck per player)

The object is to get rid of as many of the thirty-five faceup cards as you can. You may play only the cards topmost in each row at any time. By playing a card, you expose the next card for play.

Turn over the top card of your draw stack. Onto that card, you may play any card that is next in sequence, higher or lower (e.g., a 7 or a 5 on a 6). Suit and color are irrelevant. However, you may not play anything on a King.

Play as many cards as you can. There is no limit to the number that may be played in a single turn.

When you have played all the cards you can, turn over the next of the cards in the draw stack and proceed in the same manner. Continue till you have turned all seventeen cards in the draw stack. The number of cards left in the layout on the board is your score—and the lower, the better.

To play competitively, give each player a deck; see who gets the lower score.

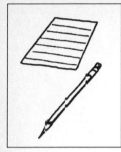

Solo Scrabble™— Version 1

MATERIALS

Scrabble™ board, paper, pen or pencil for scoring

In this game, your child utilizes the board and tiles to try to make words, scoring according to the double- and triple-word and -letter squares on the board.

Place all the letter tiles facedown and mix them up. Start by drawing ten tiles. Now make the most advantageous word you can, taking into account the bonuses offered by the various squares. Write your score down, and then draw the same number of tiles you have used so that you have ten again. Now lay down another word.

Continue in this way until you have used up all the tiles or until you cannot put down any of the tiles in your hand. There is no trading in of unusable tiles. The only way you can get a tile out of your hand is by placing it on the board. At the end, see what your score is. Since this is a solitaire game, there is no one else to beat, but you can always try to improve on your previous score or beat your personal best.

Solo Scrabble™— Version 2

ONE

MATERIALS

Scrabble™ board, paper, pen or pencil for scoring

In this game, as in the previous one, your child utilizes the board and tiles to try to make words. But unlike the first game, in this game you get a higher score for longer words while ignoring the bonus square scoring on the board. In other words, the double- and triple-word and -letter squares don't count, and neither do the point values on the letter tiles.

For every word of three, four, or five letters that you form, give yourself a point. For every six-letter word or seven-letter word, take 2 points, and 4 points for an eight-letter word. Words of nine or more letters score 7 points.

If you can create a longer word out of a shorter one on the board, you get credit for the full length of the word providing you have not merely added an ER, ED, ING, ES, or S to the end of a word. In other words, changing RUN to RUNNER or RUNNING would not be worth anything; but if you have CAT on the board and turn it into EDUCATION or if you have ROOM and turn it into ROOMMATE, you would get full credit for the word.

All the other rules in version 1 apply.

Splash!

MATERIALS

Bathing suits, balloons, water

Two (or more) friends or siblings, or a gaggle of kids from up and down the block, can converge on your backyard armed with an artillery of water balloons and have a grand (and wet!) time as the backyard explodes in a major water-balloon "battle."

For a variation, try filling one of the balloons with shaving cream (with Dad's permission!) or whipped cream (with Mom's permission!). Who will get "slimed" with the "loaded" balloon? Which balloon is it? You'll find out . . . the hard way.

En garde! Gotcha!

Stare Down

Here's an easy concept:

Simple form: Try not to be the first player to blink. Advanced form: Try to make the other player giggle before he succeeds in doing the same to you. (See also Keep a Straight Face, page 162.)

In the first form, both players simply stare at each other, trying to keep their eyes wide open. The first to give in and blink loses.

MATERIALS

✐ None

Is the second form, it's perfectly kosher to make fierce or funny faces, to cross your eyes, to do anything facial to make your opponent crack a smile. All this must be done silently, however. No talking. No weird noises. No belches, whistles, monkey sounds, jokes, riddles, or other verbal or vocal attacks. It's strictly facial.

It's definitely fun.

Start a Leaf Collection

MATERIALS

- One of each type of leaf you can find in your yard or your neighborhood

It's amazing how different one leaf looks from another. An oak leaf is distinctively an oak leaf; a maple is unquestionably a maple. Other types of leaves are perhaps less familiar, less instantaneously recognizable, but they are nonetheless distinctive.

How many different types of leaves can your child find in your neighborhood? He can confine his collection to just tree leaves or include bushes as well. If he's old enough to do a bit of researching, he can search through a library book to learn the names of the different kinds of leaves and label each leaf in his new collection. If not, he can still enjoy the leaves and take note of the distinguishing characteristics that make a poplar look different from a sycamore, a maple different from an oak.

Statues

Statues, like many other games, requires first choosing someone to be It. Unlike many other games, though, in Statues, it's quite good to be It. Each player, one at a time, stands in front of It with one arm up in the air. It takes the player's arm, swings him around in a circle, then releases the now-dizzy player. This player will likely stagger or struggle to keep his balance.

MATERIALS

✐ None

At some point within a second or a few seconds from releasing the player he spun, It yells, "Freeze!" (In some parts of the country, It yells, "Statues!" instead.) At that point, the player must freeze in whatever position he's in—complete with any dizzy grimace, bent knee or arm, whatever.

He remains in that position as It spins the next player and the next, each of whom, in turn, must freeze at It's command and remain frozen while It goes on to the next player and the next. When It has spun and frozen everyone, It surveys the group of statues and selects the one he likes best—the funniest, the most ludicrous, the hardest position to stay frozen in . . . and probably simply his best friend in some cases. That player now becomes It for the next round.

Story-Time Turnabout

TWO

MATERIALS

✐ A parent, a good book

Most bedtimes, parents, you probably read to your child, right? Just for a change one afternoon, let her read a story to you. Whether it's a book or story, or just part of one, or a poem or two, this turnabout will not only encourage your child to be a reader but also fill her with a sense of importance.

Beginning readers may need help with tough words . . . or may improvise, telling the story rather than reading it. Don't criticize: "Is that really what the page says?" This isn't a reading lesson. This isn't about how well your child deciphers C-A-T.

Older kids, too, can enjoy reading to their parents. Kids enjoy introducing their parents to books and authors the parents may not be well acquainted with. What a sense of importance to be able to teach your mom something . . . even if that "something" is simply what a neat author Judy Blume is.

A child who can be pleased and satisfied by reading after school, whatever form that reading might take, is a child whose whole life is going to be richer than the lives of people for whom picking up a book is not a natural act.

String Balloons

Your child can have fun making these really neat, pretty string balloons; they begin with regular balloons but quickly turn into something else. He'll need one real balloon for each string balloon he wants to create. Here are instructions for making one string balloon:

O N E

Blow up a balloon and tie it off. Pour some glue into a pie pan, and dip a long piece of string into the glue. When it's well covered, lift it out of the glue and hold it over the pan long enough for the excess glue to drip off. Lay the glued string onto the balloon in a swooping, whorled design. (You're looking for a sort of lacy effect, so you want curves, not sharp angles.)

Repeat the process as often as you need to so that the balloon becomes pretty well covered in an intricate design. Bits of balloon should be visible through the string here and there, but there shouldn't be any huge areas of balloon showing.

When the glue has dried, pop the balloon with a needle or pin, and you're left with a string balloon.

MATERIALS

✐ Round or oval balloons (not the long and thin ones), string or embroidery floss, glue such as Elmer's, pie tin, needle or pin, newspaper to work over

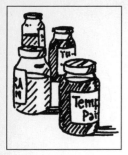

String Paintings

Tempera paints, lengths of string from 1 to 2 feet long, paper suitable for painting on, newspaper to work over

The number of strings you'll use is up to you. Each color of paint you're using will require one string. If you only have three colors of paint, the decision is easy: Unless you want to blend paint colors, you'll use three strings, one for each of the colors. If you have eight colors of tempera, consider not using all of them.

Fold the paper in half, making a sharp crease, and open it again. Dip each length of string in a different color of paint and hold it over the paint jar until it stops dripping. Now lay each string down on one side of the folded paper, letting it swoop and swirl as you ease it down to the surface. Leave the paint-free end of the string, which you were holding, extended out off the paper.

Now fold the other half of the paper over the half the strings are lying on. Press down on the top and pull slowly on the end of each string till they've all come out of the paper, making designs as they slide out. Open the paper again. There's your painting!

String Race

In this race, speed takes a back seat to "toeing the line." Since players may stagger or fall, it's advisable to play in a fairly open area.

Stretch out a 15-foot length of string and position one player at either end. The player at the "finish" end holds a stopwatch (or keeps an eye on the second hand of his watch). The third player, who is about to race, gets in position just in front of the "start" end of the string. The nonracing player at the start end spins the racer five times quickly and yells, "Go." The player at the finish end starts the timing. And the dizzy racer begins hurrying along the string to the finish line.

She may either walk or run, but if at any time she puts a foot down anywhere but on the string, she is out of the race. When she reaches the finish end of the string and steps on the very end, the player with the stopwatch notes the time.

Now she trades places with one of the others, and it's that player's turn to race. Eventually all three will take a turn. The winner is the player who completed the course in the fastest possible time without ever putting a foot down anywhere but on the string.

THREE
or more

MATERIALS

✐ 15-foot length of string, stopwatch or watch with second hand

Stuck on You!

MATERIALS

Magnets, cardboard, cement that bonds to metal (such as Duco), scissors, photos of your child, or construction paper and crayons

Your child can make magnets that Grandma (or you) will love to have on the fridge . . . because your child drew the pictures attached to them or because they have your child's picture on them. Here's what she needs to do:

Buy a few small magnets. (Try your local variety store or hardware store.) Glue either a small picture of yourself or a small picture that you've drawn to a piece of cardboard. Using a cement that bonds to metal (e.g., Duco), affix that cardboard-backed picture to the magnet.

Now your child—or her very own artwork—will smile at you every time you get near the fridge (even if you're dipping into the ice cream again).

Survey Your Street

For the mathematical-minded or statistic-oriented child, a survey conducted from a front window can be satisfying. This won't work if you live on a cul de sac, but if your street has any amount of either pedestrian or vehicular traffic, you've got the means to keep your child occupied for a while.

On a street with ample foot traffic, ask him if he thinks more men or women walk by the house in a typical half hour. Or ask him if he thinks more adults than kids walk past in that same time frame. Then challenge him to find out by observing.

On a street with mainly vehicular traffic, the possibilities are even greater for a survey—or several: Are there more cars or more trucks and other vehicles? What's the most popular color? What states are represented on the license plates besides your own? Are there more four-door or more two-door cars?

O N E
or more

MATERIALS

✐ None

Syrup Painting

MATERIALS

✐ Corn syrup, food coloring, white or pale solid color heavyweight paper plate, black marking pen, disposable cups (paper or plastic), paintbrush(es)

Sometimes the kids get bored with doing the same thing over and over. And sometimes all it takes is a small change to make them feel like they're doing something totally new.

Take painting. If you have a bored child on your hands and you suggest he get out his paints and paint a picture, he may say, "Aww, I don't feel like painting." But suggest he paint with syrup, and suddenly you're talking about a "new" activity! Go figure—but don't fight it; just get out the corn syrup and the food coloring. And . . . .

Mix a few drops of food coloring into a small paper cup close to full of syrup. Repeat for each color you want to use. Draw the outlines of a design or picture on a white or light solid color heavyweight paper plate, using a black marking pen. Now fill in the black outlines with the "syrup paint." Allow to dry and hang the plate with pride.

Be sure to wash your paintbrushes very carefully.

Talk Backward!

Can you say a whole sentence backward? I mean . . . backward sentence whole a say you can? Try carrying on a conversation with another child, with both of you saying whatever you want to say backward.

Backward sentence longer much a speak you can?

Difficult more even be will says he what to answer an forming and.

It's not easy . . . I mean, Easy not it's. It isn't, difficult it's. Ahead thinking requires it.

But it is fun! I mean, Fun is it but.

How you shown I've. It try you now.

T W O
or more

MATERIALS

✐ None

Target Rolling

MATERIALS

✐ Chalk or string, golf ball or rubber ball

Like golf, this is a good game to play either solo or in competition. And as in golf, your object is to get a ball into something . . . but in this case, instead of holes in the ground, you're aiming at circles on the ground.

If you're playing on pavement, you can draw circles on the ground with chalk; if you're playing on the grass or dirt, create your circles out of lengths of string. In either case, figure out where you're going to "tee off" from, stand there, lean down, and roll the ball at the circle. The object is to get the ball into the circle in one try. The circle should be about three times as large as the ball. The tee should be far enough from the hole that it's not ridiculously easy to score, yet not so far away that it's frustratingly impossible. The number of holes that will comprise your course depends entirely on the area you have to play in.

Tell Me a Riddle . . . of Your Own Invention

O N E
or more

MATERIALS

✐ None; or paper, pen

Who makes up all those funny, silly, laughable riddles, anyhow? Real people . . . just like you. In fact, it could be you! So why don't you try? One way is just to let your mind wander, but a more scientific approach is to think of a word that can be twisted into another word or that has two meanings.

An example: The word POP can mean "what a balloon or soda can does." It's also another word for soda. It's also another word for dad. So . . . define your father's scalp? It's . . . a pop top. [Groan.]

Okay . . . your turn!

You may want to write down your best riddles so that you don't forget them.

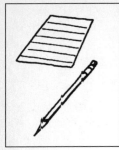

Ten to Get the Word

T W O

MATERIALS

✐ Pen, paper

How good are your sleuthing skills?
Your verbal sleuthing skills, that is.
One of the two players in this game is It
and has to guess the Secret Word, which
the other player chooses. The opposition
player's word must consist of four letters,
two of which he writes down on a sheet of
paper, drawing dashes in the position the
other two letters would appear in. (If the
Secret Word is POST, the opposition player
might write P O _ _ or _ O S _—there is
no rule as to which letters he writes down.)
The Secret Word may not be a proper
noun. The player who is It now has ten
questions in which to guess the Secret
Word.

The nature of these questions is open
ended. That is, It may guess at a letter: "Is
there an E?" He may try to guess the
nature of the word: "Is it the name of a
flower?" He may guess the part of speech:
"Is it a verb?"

If, in ten tries, It succeeds in guessing
the Secret Word, he wins. If not, the
opposition player wins. Either way, they
trade places, with the former It becoming
the opposition and the former opposition
player now becoming It for a new round.

Themed Chain

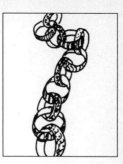

Most kids know how to make chains from an early age, but instead of using the usual construction paper, these chains are fashioned from themed gift wrap. For a Christmas chain, use last year's used-and-folded-away Christmas gift wrap, in reds and greens and with Santas and snowmen and other appropriate images. For birthdays, use gift wrap with birthday images.

O N E

MATERIALS

✐ Scissors
(beginner's
scissors are
okay), gift wrap,
glue

Cut strips of paper of pretty uniform length. A good size is from ¾ to one 1 wide and around 7 inches long. Pick up one strip and bring one end just over the other, creating a circle with the printing on the outside. Glue an area of perhaps ¼ inch on the underside of the top end, the end you've folded over the other end, to hold the circle together. You have now created one link in the chain.

Now select another strip, preferably one cut from a contrasting piece of gift wrap. Slip this strip through the first circle and bring the ends together in the same fashion, gluing them together so that the two circles are linked. You have the beginning of a chain. Continue in this manner, interlinking circles till you have quite a length of varicolored links.

317

Themed Wastebasket

MATERIALS

✎ Photos, magazine pictures, old greeting cards, pictures from any other source that depict a particular theme (such as sports or animals or cars)

Your child can turn an ordinary, boring wastebasket into something she'll actually get pleasure out of.

She needs to save all pictures she can get her hands on that depict her area of interest—horses, animals in general, sports, boats, or whatever. The larger the picture, the better. I don't mean 10 by 17 inches, but a 1-by-1-inch picture is likely to get lost in this project. Where a whole picture depicts the theme, she can cut the whole picture out. In other cases, she should cut around the horse, the car, the kitten, and the fish and eliminate the background.

When she has amassed quite a collection of suitable pictures, she glues them onto the wastebasket, collage-style, with one picture overlapping another.

She can save those smaller pictures and use them to cover a jar for use as a matching pencil holder.

This Is My Universe

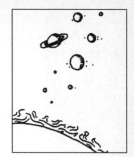

One more item is needed that's not specified under Materials: a good imagination. For this fun activity, kids can pretend either that they've arrived from another planet or that they've blasted off from Earth into space and discovered this other planet. But in either case, your young explorer is asked to provide, in a combination of words and pictures, as much of the following as he wants:

ONE
or more

MATERIALS

✐ Paper, pen or pencil or crayons or fine-line markers

Descriptions of the inhabitants of the planet, both the people—if that's the right word for them—and the animals, as well as the plant life. Descriptions of the clothes the planet's people wear. Descriptions of the food they eat and perhaps what the animals eat too. Descriptions of the holidays celebrated on the planet, what these commemorate, and how they're celebrated. Descriptions of the sky as it's visible from that planet—the stars and constellations and planets that can be seen in this other universe. Names and descriptions of the other planets in that universe. An explanation of the planet's political system. Descriptions of flags, money, postage stamps, and anything else that might be of interest to us poor Earthlings stuck here on this planet.

Thread-Spool Puppets

MATERIALS

Empty thread spools, pencil, paint or marking pens, glue, yarn or crepe paper or cotton, construction paper

Here's another kind of puppet (also see Puppet Theatre, pages 257 and 258) your child can make, one that requires minimal dexterity to create. An empty spool of thread becomes the puppet's head; draw the face on with fine-line colored markers, or use paint. Give the puppet hair by gluing yarn, cotton (for white hair), or crepe paper to the top of the spool.

Sharpen a pencil (to thin the shaft so that it will fit in the hole in the spool), and glue the pencil into the bottom of the spool. Give your puppet a body by cutting a shirt, dress, or other clothing out of construction paper and gluing it onto the front of the pencil. If you wish, you can cut little hands out of flesh-toned construction paper and glue them to the ends of the puppet's sleeves, though this isn't essential.

Make several different puppets, and you're ready to put on a show, either acting out a favorite story or simply having the puppets ad lib a dialogue with each other or with the audience.

Throwing Money Around

Though this is more fun as a competitive game, it can also be played as a solo. The procedure is simple: The player—we'll assume there's one player for now—stands behind a line perhaps a foot from the empty coffee can and throws the coins. The more coins he gets into the can, the more money he scores. The final score is counted in terms of monetary value . . . that is, he doesn't score "six coins," he scores "$1.02." To beat his previous score next time, he has to score more money—perhaps by sinking five quarters and a dime, instead of three quarters, two dimes, a nickel, and two pennies, as he did to score $1.02.

The same is true in a competitive game: The winner isn't the child who scores the largest number of coins but rather the child who scores the coins with the largest dollar value.

O N E
or more

MATERIALS

Empty coffee can, assorted coins

Tie-Dyed Paper Towels

MATERIALS

White paper
towels, muffin tin
or bowls, water,
food coloring,
newspapers to
work over and to
dry the towels on

You'll use no rubber bands and no T-shirts for this tie-dyeing project—and you'll do no tying either—but the results will be colorful, distinctive, and attractive.

Start by putting water in at least four bowls or four cups of a muffin tin. (Food coloring sets have four colors, but you can mix colors or dilute them to different strengths for different hues, and so your child can wind up with as many bowls or muffin cups of colored water as you'll allow.)

Now take a piece of paper towel and dip a corner into a bowl of one color. Dip each corner and various areas of the middle in as many different and contrasting colors as you wish; the color will, of course, spread through the absorbent paper. Spread the paper towel out on newspaper to dry while you tie-dye another one.

These can be hung on the wall as decoration, used as dollhouse bedspreads or tablecloths, or even used to wrap small gifts.

Timed Stroll

How's your sense of time? Do you have a pretty fair idea of when a minute is up? The object of this challenge is to walk across a room in exactly one minute. How close can you come? Strolling slowly, taking as small and slow steps as you want, try to take exactly a minute to cross a room.

 O N E
or more

MATERIALS

✐ Stopwatch or watch with second hand

Players may not look at their watches (and should cover or turn any clock in the room so that they can't see it), but it's permissible for them to count in their heads (e.g., One Mississippi, two Mississippi) in any form of timing that helps them.

A solo player should just challenge himself to come as close to exactly a minute as he can . . . and then do better next time. Two or more players can play competitively if they wish, trying to see who gets the closest, or they can simply each try to better his own personal best.

Today's Events—in Pictures

MATERIALS

🖍 Paper, crayons or paints or marking pens

Almost every child has at least one grandma somewhere—and often not a mere local phone call away. Grandma wants to know what her darling has been up to, but Junior may not yet be proficient at writing. When you have to stop to ask Mom to spell every third word in your letter, writing to Grandma about the day's events becomes significantly less fun.

So how about drawing her a picture? Your child may have trouble spelling out the words in a sentence like this: We had a jump-rope contest on the playground at lunch hour and I did Teddy Bear perfectly and won! But she can draw it! Grandma may not understand perfectly the significance of a proud, grinning, rope-jumping stick figure, but she's bound to know it's good news, she'll treasure the drawing, and she'll glory in it all the more when her next phone conversation with you or your offspring reveals the full significance of the picture.

When Grandma calls, she can always prompt, "Tell me about the picture of the dog. What was that all about?" and elicit a flood of words from her previously reticent grandchild.

Tongue Twisters

The most well-known tongue twisters are probably "Peter Piper picked a peck of pickled peppers" and "She sells sea shells by the sea shore." But there are many other sentences or phrases that are just as difficult to say at all, let alone ten times, quickly.

Trying your hand—or rather, your mouth—at these verbal monstrosities is fun enough; trying to dream others up is even more fun.

Two kids (or more) can have fun together seeing who can repeat a tongue twister the most number of times before messing up. They can invent tongue twisters and see how well each other does with them. They can be very competitive about it or just have fun together.

But even one child by himself can have a fun time repeating "Silly Caesar seized his snifter, stiffly sniffed, and sneezed" ten times and trying not to get his tongue tangled in the process.

"Lemon liniment is a truly rural cure." Can you say that ten times quickly?

ONE
or more

MATERIALS

✐ None

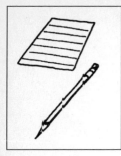

O N E
or more

MATERIALS

✐ Paper, pen or pencil

Top Ten Lists

Letterman isn't the only person with Top Ten lists. Your child can get in on the action. The results of his attempts are likely to be a bit sophomoric, but what do you expect at age eight or eleven? You may need to suggest a few list topics to get him started: Top Ten Things That Are Wrong with the School Lunches; Top Ten Annoying Teacher Habits; Top Ten Things That Are Wrong with TV; Top Ten Excuses for Handing in Homework Late. Then just turn him loose and let him start writing.

Who knows . . . your child may have a future as a TV comedy writer!

Top Ten Rules of . . . .

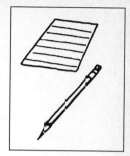

What are the top ten rules for being a good parent? Wouldn't it be interesting to see what your child came up with? Suppose you restricted her so that nothing frivolous was permissible (e.g., "Serve cake at every meal, even breakfast")? She might actually make a list you could learn something from. (And she, in thinking about whether a rule was realistic and feasible, might learn something too.)

What are the top ten rules for being a good teacher? I'll bet she has something to say on that subject, too. And here's one she herself can learn from: What are the top ten rules for being a good friend?

What other categories can she think of to devise such rules for?

O N E

MATERIALS

✐ Paper, pen or pencil

MATERIALS

✐ Paper, pencil with eraser

Town Planner

What's the best part about your town's layout? The ice cream store's location right next to the school? What's the worst part about your town's layout? The long distance to the school from your house?

Ask your child to draw a new layout for your town—or part of the town—the way she'd like to see it. Suppose she could build the town all over . . . how would she do it? You can either specify that the streets have to be the same as they are now or let her lay out a whole new grid of streets. Maybe she'd like them radiating out in spokes, like in Washington, D.C. Or maybe your town isn't composed of an even grid of parallel streets and intersecting perpendicular ones, and she thinks it would be easier to find her way around if all the streets were in such a fashion.

Town-in-a-Hubcap

Place dirt, potting soil, or sand in a hubcap or pie pan. This is where your child will construct a part of a small world . . . a town all his own. Using pipe cleaners and/or construction paper and/or cardboard, and coloring with crayons where appropriate, your child can make houses, flowers, trees, skyscrapers, cars, people, and anything else he cares to fill his little world with.

O N E

Since this is already a mixed-media project, he can feel free to add toy plastic figures, Monopoly™ houses, or any other additions that fit within the scale he's working in. He may even find himself digging in the backyard or the nearby woods for weeds that would be the perfect size for tall trees in his newly created world. Got moss somewhere nearby? Doesn't it make a fine golf course or lawn? Bury a small jar lid (mushrooms? baby food?) in the dirt and fill it with water—instant lake.

MATERIALS

✐ Dirt or potting soil or sand, hubcap or metal pie pan, pipe cleaners, construction paper, cardboard, scissors, crayons

MATERIALS

One tennis ball or
rubber ball, ten
toilet paper tubes

T-P Bowling

As with real bowling, T-P bowling can be played by one solo player or by a pair or group, and if played by multiple players, they can compete against each other or each simply try to do his best.

Your bowling pins are empty T-P tubes; your bowling ball is a rubber ball or tennis ball. Set the T-P tubes up in standard bowling-pin configuration, with a very small space separating each of the tubes from each tube next to it. Stand behind a lag line about 10 feet from the pins and roll the ball. Throwing or bouncing the ball is not permitted.

Unlike regulation bowling, you only get one ball per frame; there are no spares. Score 1 point for each tube you knock down, and take a 10-point bonus for a strike (knocking all ten pins down with one ball). In other words, for getting all ten with one ball, you'd score 20 (one point for each pin, plus a 10-point bonus).

Bowl ten frames (roll at the complete setup ten times) for a full game, as in regulation bowling.

T-P Dachshunds

Punch two holes close to each other at one end of the T-P tube and another two close together at the other end. Thread a brown pipe cleaner through each pair of holes so that the two ends of each pipe cleaner extend down through each of the pair of holes; these are your dog's four legs. Halfway around the tube from one pair of legs, punch another hole and insert another pipe cleaner, for the tail.

Draw one side of the dog's head on construction paper, including ears and features. Cut the head out and draw the features that belong on the other side as well, then tape the head to the tube.

You now have one dachshund. You can create a whole kennelful, with enough T-P tubes . . . and T-P tubes are one commodity a family always seems to have a steady supply of!

These dogs won't chew up your homework, either.

O N E

MATERIALS

✐ Toilet paper tube, construction paper, scissors, crayons, tape (such as Scotch Tape), three brown pipe cleaners, hole punch

331

Trade-a-Book

MATERIALS

✎ Books, paper, pen or pencil

We all know what happens when you lend a book: Often you don't get it back; when you do, it's not always in as good a condition as it was when you lent it; and in order to get it back, you often have to keep after the borrower.

First, make bookplates for all your books. (See Make Bookplates, page 180.) Or, as an alternative, get a rubber stamp with PROPERTY OF [YOUR NAME] or THIS BOOK BELONGS TO [YOUR NAME] on it. A simple rubber stamp (not the self-inking kind) costs only a few dollars.

Next, make a list of all your books. And, if you have access to a copying machine, or a computer (on which you can type something just once and print it out perhaps ten times), make a bunch of copies of your list.

Then offer the list around to your friends, and tell them you'll be happy to lend books to them . . . provided each friend lends a book to you in return.

You'll get to read a lot of books that way . . . and because you're holding your friends' books, they'll be more likely to return your books to you.

332

Treat Hunt

Instead of your child coming home and finding a plate of cookies on the table or helping herself to cookies from the box, suppose you said, "You may have the cookies . . . as soon as you can find them"? Hide the cookies, or raisins, or bananas in places that will be neither too difficult nor too easy to find. Too easy takes the fun out; too difficult is frustrating to a hungry child.

Establish ground rules: "There are no cookies hidden in your brother's room, in our dresser drawers, in your dad's workshop"—wherever you want to declare Out of Bounds.

Younger children are likely to want to return the favor and to hide some cookies for you to hunt after they've found what you hid. If it's even remotely practicable, let it happen. You'll be touched and amazed to discover in a few years how enormously important this kind of memory is for your child.

It's kind of like an Easter egg hunt—except the treats are much more delicious than eggs . . . and it isn't even Easter.

O N E

with parental preparation

MATERIALS

⌀ The child's daily ration of after-school cookies or raisins or fruit rolls or other treats that might be the order of the day in your family

333

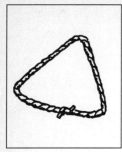

Triangular Tug-of-War

MATERIALS

✎ A 3-yard length of rope whose ends have been tied together, three handkerchiefs or rags or tissues or pieces of cloth

Each player holds onto the rope at approximately one third of the way around the rope from each of the other players so that when they tug on the rope, it forms approximately an equilateral triangle. A handkerchief (or similar item) is placed on the ground, just beyond the reach of each of the players.

At the word GO, each of the players tries to pick up his handkerchief without letting go of the rope. The first player to succeed is the winner, but if you drop the rope, you're out of the game.

A Trip from the Moon

Here's a bit of creative thinking that's fun to think about on your own, to discuss with friends, and even to write your thoughts about on paper. Here's the question:

Suppose there used to be people living on the moon . . . or on Mars? Who were they? What would life have been like for them? Why do you suppose they no longer live there? What do you suppose happened to them?

You can take this creative-thinking fun as far as you want, including drawing pictures of what their homes and other buildings might have looked like and what the people themselves might have looked like. (We're assuming they didn't come from the Earth originally, so they may not have looked like us at all.)

You can even invent a language they might have used.

O N E
or more

MATERIALS

✐ None; or paper, pen or pencil

335

A Trip to the Moon

ONE
or more

MATERIALS

Paper, pen or pencil

It may not be that many more years before we of the Earth establish a colony on the moon. And beyond that . . . who knows? . . . we might even colonize Mars.

Here's a chance to start all over. As wonderful as life on Earth can be, we've got our problems down here, too. One country fights against another; and most of us are pretty careless of the planet we call home, whether it's a person carelessly tossing a candy wrapper onto the ground or a company causing a huge amount of pollution with their factory.

What's a good list of rules to govern the settlers who colonize the moon or Mars? If we're going to start all over again, let's do it right this time.

You write the rules!

Two-Card Drop

As in Flipping Cards (page 93), the object here is to win all your opponent's cards—or as many as you can win within a fixed time. But here the object is to capture your opponent's card by touching it.

Player 1 starts and flips or simply drops a card. Player 2 now drops a card, trying to touch Player 1's card. If he succeeds, he collects both cards. If he misses, Player 1 picks the two cards up. Now Player 2 drops a card first, and this time Player 1 tries to drop his card so that it touches Player 2's card. Again, if he succeeds—if any part of his card touches Player 2's card—he wins both cards; but if he misses, Player 2 gets to pick up both cards.

The game is over either when one player has cleaned out the other or when a preset amount of time is over, in which case the player with the most cards is declared the winner.

T W O

MATERIALS

📓 A deck of cards

✂ Optional: Two decks

337

Unlocking the Secret

MATERIALS

An old deadbolt
lock, screwdriver

Kids who have a mechanical mind (whose number are legion) or an inquisitive mind (and that encompasses most kids) will be fascinated by taking apart an ordinary deadbolt lock to see how it works. The workings of the mechanism are fairly evident once the lock has been disassembled.

The child may even be able to reassemble the lock by himself, but if not, never fear; in all probability, you can reassemble it. The interior of such locks is relatively simple to reassemble or repair. (And you didn't take the lock off the front door for him to play with . . . did you?)

Your child will be thrilled to feel knowledgeable about what happens when the key is turned to lock or unlock the front door. In addition, you'll be doing him another favor: You'll get him started in thinking of household repairs as being well within the competence of ordinary people.

Unlucky Fives

The cards are played facedown, since number and suit are irrelevant. Each player starts with twenty-five poker chips (again, color is irrelevant) and five cards, spread out in front of him so that everyone can see how many he has. The remaining cards are placed in a draw pile.

The first player rolls the die and draws that number of cards, placing them in front of him, spread out. He counts his total cards.

At any point during the game, if a player has exactly five cards, he pays a one-chip penalty to the bank. If a player has exactly ten, he pays a two-chip penalty. And if a player has fifteen or more cards in his hand, he is "bankrupt" and out of the game.

The first player now rolls a second time and returns the specified number of cards to the draw pile. Again, he pays any penalty called for. That ends his turn.

If the second die roll of a turn would obligate a player to return more cards than he has, he gives up all his cards but is not out of the game. On his next turn, he will draw normally and does not "owe" the "deficit" from the previous turn.

The last player left in the game still holding chips is the winner.

TWO
or more

MATERIALS

✐ A die, deck of cards (incomplete deck is okay), twenty-five poker chips per player

Uno, Dos, Tres . . .

O N E
or more

MATERIALS

✏ A book or two on foreign languages

If your child is like most, he'll love to be in possession of Important Information . . . like how to talk in a Real Foreign Language. While I'm not suggesting a whole Berlitz course, or anything that's going to feel like (ugh!) homework, learning to count in a foreign language shouldn't bring on a major brain strain and will be considered Genuine Fun by most kids.

If your high school or college French, Spanish, or German hasn't flown totally out the window, that's a good place to start. And foreign language dictionaries or the Internet can provide further help.

If he really gets into learning to count in several languages, teach him the days of the week in as many languages as you can muster up the info on . . . and perhaps add the months, and maybe the seasons too.

Your child will probably throw himself into memorizing the numbers, days of the week, and so on with so much eagerness that you'll have to spend an hour practicing restraint to prevent yourself from launching into your If You Put This Much Effort Into Your Homework You'd Be At Harvard Before Your Tenth Birthday speech.

Untrue—in Any Words

"**T**hat's a lie." "That's bull." Those are fighting words. To call something "a lie," even if it is, often provokes a fight . . . the more so if the person saying it didn't mean to lie. And "bull" is short for a longer word that's Not Acceptable in most households. "That's a lot of nonsense" is more polite . . . but how many other ways are there to say the same thing politely?

"That's hogwash" is an old-fashioned but socially acceptable expression. Personally, I like "Horsefeathers!" There's no such thing as horsefeathers . . . so the expression implies there's no such thing as what the speaker just said, either.

Can you think of more colorful expressions that call a load of untruth just that . . . but in words that won't offend? How many ways can you find to label a statement untrue politely?

O N E
or more

MATERIALS

✐ None; or paper, pen or pencil

Vegetable Prints

MATERIALS

Tempera paint, paper towels, paring knife, typing paper, assorted vegetables (such as parsley, potatoes, broccoli, carrots, celery)

This activity is genuinely messy . . . so you know kids will love it. And they'll create something pretty looking . . . so you know Grandma will love displaying the results.

Start by making one or more homemade, nonpermanent ink pads. Do this by soaking a folded-over piece of paper towel with tempera paint, one piece of towel for each color you want to use.

Cut the veggies. A sliced celery stalk will give a C-shaped, or swoopy, impression; a carrot will produce a circle or oval, depending on how you slice it. (How about one of each?) The parsley and broccoli will give outrageous designs. And potatoes have been used by kids as ink stamps for generations—they can be cut to form letters (e.g., a child's initials), stars, exclamation points, or whatever grabs your child's fancy.

By combining the impressions from different vegetables and by using different colors, your child can create a rather complex and striking design on a sheet of white typing paper.

Now . . . ready, set, stamp!

Very Icy

Does your child beg for ices or ice cream while you cringe and wish she were craving something more nutritious? There's a solution to make both of you happy . . . and she gets the added bonus of having some fun, too.

Your child can make her own juice-sicles, then eat them when she craves ices. Meanwhile, you'll know she's eating frozen fruit juice, so you'll be happy too. Here's all she has to do to make juice-sicles when she gets home from school today . . . and she'll have them to eat tomorrow:

Pour fruit juice into small paper or plastic cups. Cover each cup with aluminum foil or plastic wrap and make a slit in the middle of the wrap just large enough to insert a Popsicle stick. Insert the stick, then put the cups in the freezer till they're frozen solid.

Making the juice-sicles is fun and easy . . . and consuming the results isn't exactly a chore either!

O N E

MATERIALS

⬭ Fruit juice, small paper or plastic cups, aluminum foil or plastic wrap, Popsicle sticks

343

Very Short Stories

TWO
or more

MATERIALS

✐ Paper, pen or pencil

In this fun game, each participant contributes to the creation of a very short "story"—with hilarious results. Here's how to play a two-handed game:

Player 1 writes the name of a man or boy at the top of a sheet of paper and folds the paper over so that Player 2 can't see what she's written. The person should be someone known—personally or by reputation—to both players. It might be a boy in school, a historical figure like George Washington, or a fictional character such as Tarzan. Player 2 writes "met" and the name of a woman or girl, again known to both players.

Player 2 folds the paper over again and hands it back to Player 1, who writes "at" or "in" or "on" and then a place: "on the moon," "in the lunchroom," "in the bathtub," "at the Olympics." She folds the paper and hands it back to Player 2, who writes, "He said," and then attributes a sentence to the male (whose identity she doesn't know). Player 1 now adds, "She said," again without knowing who the person is. Player 2 ends with "So they," finishing with what the two of them did. Then one of the players unfolds the page and reads the "story" aloud.

344

Walnut Mice

The walnut shell is the mouse's body. Start your mouse's face by drawing two large dots with the marker at one end, for the eyes. Cut ears and a nose out of felt, and glue them in the appropriate places. Use bristles from an old brush or broom for whiskers, cutting them if you need to in order to get them the right length. Glue two on each side of the nose.

Cut a strip of yarn about 4 inches long and glue it to the other end, for a tail.

I don't think you'll fool any cats with these mice, but they're awfully cute decorations . . . and they won't get into your cheese supply.

ONE

MATERIALS

Walnut shells, glue, scissors, yarn (grey, brown, or black), felt scraps (same colors as yarn), black marker, bristles from an old brush or broom

Waxed Garfield?

MATERIALS

✐ Comic strips
(preferably
though not
essentially in
color), waxed
paper, spoon

Place a piece of waxed paper over a picture from the comic pages (or a comic book). Using the edge (not the rounded base) of a spoon, rub over the picture. Be sure to rub all of the picture, or you'll wind up minus one of Garfield's paws, Snoopy's nose, or Marmaduke's tail. By the same token, don't rub over anything you don't want to capture on the waxed paper, or you'll have inadvertently included part of a tree, half of a person, or the edge of the next panel. Rub firmly, though be careful not to tear the paper.

Remember that whatever you pick up will come out reversed.

With a little practice, you'll eventually be ready to make composite strips. By rubbing over Garfield, then positioning Snoopy next to him and rubbing over that, then adding Marmaduke in the blank space adjoining, you can create quite a menagerie of comic strip canines and felines . . . or a playground full of comic strip kids, or any other sort of composite you want.

Weekly Wrap-Up

" **I**'ll never forget the look on your face when I showed you the A I got in history!" your child may say to you, yet it's likely in time he'll forget both the look and even getting that A . . . unless he has something to jog his memory.

That's where a weekly wrap-up comes in. In it, your child can record the significant events of the family's week— his and the other family members'. Did one of your kids get an honor in school? Did you get a promotion at work? Did a child participate in a school assembly or a karate demonstration? Did somebody learn to ride a bike or get a driver's license? It's all suitable for recording in the Weekly Wrap-Up.

What do you do with your Weekly Wrap-Up? Well, first of all, you can make a copy and send it to Grandma to keep her posted on family happenings. Besides that, shelve the Wrap-Ups where they can be referred to any time someone wants to reminisce. The peeks back can even be an organized event: The family can decide, on a night when nobody has plans with friends, to curl up in front of the fireplace and take a trip down memory lane.

Who says you can't time-travel?

ONE
or more

MATERIALS

Paper, pen or typewriter or computer

347

What Do You Say to That?

This is a "pretending" game in which you suddenly take on a different identity and expect your child to answer a question, either as who he really is or taking on a different identity himself.

For instance, you might say to your child, "Mr. President, we really like your country, but tell me what you think is your nation's greatest achievement?" Or you might say, "Earthling, this is a fascinating planet. What are the ten most interesting sights we ought to see while we're visiting here?" Or: "Master, you have rubbed the lamp and summoned me forth. What are your three wishes?" A related one: "As the official Pink Fairy, I am empowered to give you an extra set of hands. Now . . . what are you going to do with four hands?"

What's in a Name?

Writers know that the names they give their characters are important. People reading a book about a man named Johannes Q. Hockenfuster have some idea, right from the beginning, about what Johannes is likely to be like. If the character's name is Lucretia Smythe, the fact that she's a woman isn't all that's likely to be different. And if a character's name is simply Bill Green or Sue Johnson, that brings still a different picture to mind.

Among real people, too, names count for something. Though very few people go so far as to change their first names, they do often ask that people call them by one nickname or another . . . or not call them by a certain nickname.

Take a person (or fictional character) named Katherine. She might be known by her full first name. She might be Kathy. She might be Kate, or Katie, or Kitty. Each of these brings a different image to mind.

Think about characters you might one day write stories about . . . either for school or just for fun. What are some good names for characters? What does each name make you think about that person, even before you describe him or her on paper?

ONE
or more

MATERIALS

✐ None

Who Was That Masked Man?

MATERIALS

✐ Old family photo
albums

On a day when you've got some time free to interact with your child after school, drag out those photo albums that go further back than his memory does . . . back into Ancient History when you were a child yourself, or at least to a time he can't remember.

Going through old pictures can reinforce your child's grasp of both family history and family relationships. A picture of you and Aunt Holly in your party clothes in front of your childhood home, holding (a much younger version of) Grandma's hand will bring several realities home to your child: that you and Aunt Holly were once kids yourselves, that Aunt Holly is your sister . . . and that Grandma is your—and Aunt Holly's—mom!

Tell stories, not just from your past, but from your parents' histories. One of the most important rivets of personal and of family identity is a sense of continuity and connection with the past; be sure that your child gets the knowledge of, love for, interest in, and respect for the people who made the family, and therefore your child's world, what it is.

Whoozit Boxes

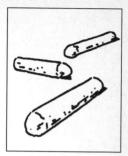

On the sidewalk, use chalk to draw two boxes side by side, two beyond that touch them, and so on, for a total of five pairs. Each box should be around twice as large as a player's foot.

The boxes are hopped through in the following order: First the nearest box on the right, then the box just beyond that, and so on to the end; then the box next to that one; then the next-nearest box coming back on the left side, and so on. Write a category in each box, such as Countries, Actors, Dogs, Cars.

The first player stands behind a starting line, perhaps 4 feet back from the boxes, and tosses his playing piece at the first box.

If it lands correctly, she hops on one foot through each box (including the first) in order, without stepping on any lines or hopping off the playing field. In each box, she calls out an example of that category that she hasn't already used. Once during each round, a player may call "Whoozit!" instead of a category.

If she gets through successfully, she now tosses her playing piece at the second square. Whenever she messes up, it becomes the next player's turn.

The player who completes the whole board first wins.

TWO
or more

MATERIALS

✐ Chalk, one playing piece (such as a button or a stone) per player

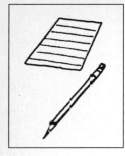

With a Critical Eye

MATERIALS

- Paper, pen or pencil
- Optional: Newspaper

Here's an activity that is fun, and is an exercise in writing, and will get your child to think more critically about the shows he sees on TV. Very simply, have him write a review of his favorite show . . . or reviews of several shows.

If he's not familiar with the format of a review, he ought to read a few in the local paper (or a magazine). He doesn't need to read reviews of TV shows, necessarily; reviews of movies or even stage shows will give him the idea. When he's conversant with the way a review is written, let him watch a few shows with a critical eye, then write reviews of them.

Every child likes to be in a position of authority, whether it's playing teacher or being the leader of a game, and writing a review may make him feel important too. Even better, he may never look at a TV show quite as uncritically again.

A Wonderful Invention

At five, or eight, or eleven, your child is probably too young to invent anything significant, but that shouldn't stop her from trying—there are exceptions to most rules, although parallel lines will never meet. Anyhow, even if your child can't draw a practical, working plan for a new invention, she can perhaps think of the idea for one. What invention does this world need?

Maybe her idea will be something simple like a book bag on wheels, in the manner of wheeled suitcases—very useful on days when you have to bring home your books from every single class plus four heavy tomes from the library. Maybe her idea will be something a bit more complex, like a bed that rises and lowers on stilts. By day, the bed moves up at the touch of a button, loft-like, giving floor space underneath to play in. By night, clear the floor and push the button, and the bed lowers for easy access.

Your child may not have the practical knowledge needed to make her invention work, but if she has the idea, that's half the battle.

What is your child going to invent tomorrow?

O N E
or more

MATERIALS

✎ None; or paper, pen or pencil

353

Word Baffle

MATERIALS

✐ Dictionary

Here's a great way to encourage your child to expand her vocabulary . . . in the guise of trying to stump Mom and Dad. Your child's mission: to find a word in the dictionary each day that she doesn't think you know. She memorizes the word, its spelling, and its definition. Then she presents the word at dinnertime. Do you know the word? Can you define it? Use it in a sentence?

But keep track of the week's words, parents, because at the end of the week, it's time to turn the tables. Present all the week's words to your child and see if she remembers the meaning and the spelling of each word she challenged you with.

Word Chains

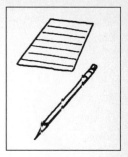

To make a word chain, take two words of the same number of letters as each other and try to "turn one word into the other." You do this by changing one letter at a time without rearranging any letters.

As an example, try to turn BEAN into STAR. Here's one way: BEAN to BEAR to SEAR to STAR. A MOON can become a FORT. How? Simple: MOON to LOON to LOOT to FOOT to FORT. Now let's try a five-letter word: Turn HEART into BOARD. I can do it in three steps: HEART to HEARD to BEARD (or HOARD) to board.

Word chains are usually a solo activity, but your child can have fun with word chains with a friend, too. The two of them decide on two words (or you can choose the two words), and then they try to puzzle out the best way to change one word into the other. The "winner" can be the one who effects the change most rapidly or the one who accomplishes it in the fewest steps.

O N E
or more

MATERIALS

Paper, pen or pencil

Word Lightning

TWO

MATERIALS

✎ Watch with second hand

Sixty seconds is your limit . . . to think of as many words as you can that begin with a given letter. Can you beat your opponent's score?

Player 1 says, "S," or "B," or perhaps "C," then quickly looks at her watch and says "Go." Player 2 immediately starts spouting as many words as he can think of that begin with the letter she's given him. Different verb forms ("ran," "run") don't count, nor do singulars and plurals ("girl," "girls" or "man," "men"); but other forms of the same word are fine ("judge" and "judgment" or "build" [the verb] and "building" [the noun]).

While Player 1 keeps track of the elapsing sixty seconds, she also needs to listen to the words that Player 2 is calling out so that she can keep track of the number he has thought of and can catch any repetitions. At the end of the minute, she calls "Time!" and announces his score.

Then they trade places; he announces a letter, calls "Go!" and keeps track of the words she comes up with.

The player with the most words wins.

Out of fair play, the letters Q, U, V, W, X, Y, and Z are not permitted.

Word Pictures

Have you ever thought of writing a word in a way that suggests the meaning of the word? It won't work with most words, but it will with some. For instance, the word SMILE can be written with the M dipping below the level of the S, the I below that, the L curving up again, and the E on the level of the S, so that the whole word is curved in a suggestion of a smile.

The word FAT can be written in letters that are exaggeratedly broad, suggesting girth. The letters of the word CURVE can be written on a curve. The letters of the word RISE can proceed upward on the page, rising.

First suggest that your child try her hand at writing those four words in that manner. Now . . . what other words can she turn into word pictures?

O N E
or more

MATERIALS

✐ Paper, pencil

357

Word Search

Word search can be played by one player or any number. The basic principle is simply to see how many smaller words you can make out of the letters in a longer word. For instance, from the word CONGRATULATE, you can get great, grate, corn, con, glue, teal, tan, ran, run, gun, gnu, ten, tongue, later, late, eat, ate, tea, lute, nog, cog, cot, tog, rung, rang, rant, runt, rent, rate, gate, goat, and more . . . you've got the idea by now.

You can give one child playing alone a specific challenge: "Can you make ten real words out of the letters in MULTIPLICATION?" Or you can give him a more open-ended challenge: "How many words can you get out of the letters in ELEMENTARY?"

When two or more kids play together, play is usually competitive. Set them up with a stopwatch or timer and a dictionary to find big words in, and turn them loose on their own. The child who makes the most small words out of each big word wins that round. Each round is a separate game.

Word Search— Variations

Follow the instructions for the previous game, with the following exceptions:

Variation 1: At the end of each round, players compare the words they've found. Any word that's been found by more than one player gets crossed out. Players receive credit only for valid words that nobody else found.

Variation 2: Kids are credited for all valid words they find, but they receive 1 point for each two- or three-letter word, 2 points for a four-letter word, 3 points for a five-letter word, 5 points for anything larger. Each round can be a game by itself, or the scores may be kept cumulatively, with the first player to score 50 points declared the winner.

O N E
One (noncompetitive) or more (competitive)

MATERIALS

✐ Paper, pen or pencil for each player, timer or stopwatch or watch with second hand.

✄ Optional: Dictionary

359

Write a Patriotic Song

MATERIALS

✎ Paper, pen or pencil

You probably can't write music, but maybe you can write the lyrics (words) to a song. Did you know that the tune of "The Star-Spangled Banner" originally belonged to another song, called "To Anachreon in Heaven," before Francis Scott Key wrote new lyrics to the existing tune? You can do the same . . . write new lyrics to an existing song. Or write a new verse for a song.

It's best to choose old songs that are no longer copyrighted. This is true of most (but not all) patriotic songs. (For instance, "America the Beautiful" and "The Star-Spangled Banner" are not under copyright, but "God Bless America" still is.)

Why not write new words—or a new verse to add to the existing ones—for "America" ("My Country 'Tis of Thee")? Or why not write the words for a patriotic song to the tune of "Oh, Susannah" or "Old Folks at Home" ("Way Down Upon the Swannee River")?

And, of course, if you can write music, you can always tackle the tough problem of that high note in our national anthem. Maybe it's time someone wrote a new tune for Francis Scott Key's lyrics!

Write Commercials

Kids are exposed to a barrage of advertising on all but the Public TV channels. They're surely experts at listening to and watching them . . . and they probably have picked up some knowledge of how to write one from having seen so many. While I doubt your offspring could get hired by a Madison Avenue firm at this stage, I'll bet your child can write a passable advertisement for . . . well, what *is* he going to write an ad for?

ONE
or more

MATERIALS

Paper, pen or pencil

Does he have a lemonade stand, or some comic books for sale? Can he think of a funny product he can write a funny ad for? Perhaps an invisibility cream you can rub on when bullies approach so that you disappear and they can't harass you. Perhaps an Instant Homework machine that does your work for you. Perhaps the report cards for kids to give teachers. (See A Report Card for Your Teacher, page 267.)

After he writes the commercial down, he can perform it for you.

361

Yarn Vase

MATERIALS

✐ Clean jar, colorful yarn, white glue, scissors, bowl, newspaper to work over

Make a pretty vase by winding colorful yarn around a clean, empty jar. Be sure the jar is clean and dry, and precut your yarn into workable lengths. You may want to use all one color or several different ones.

Pour white glue into a bowl, and dip the yarn into the bowl, one piece at a time. Starting at the top of the jar, wrap the yarn around, pushing each strand up so that it's tight to the strand above it. As each strand is in place, dip another strand of yarn in the glue and add it to what's already on the jar.

When you reach the bottom, and you're sure there's no part of the jar showing between the yarn strands, let the jar dry and . . . presto! You have a pretty vase.

The (Your Name) Dictionary

What do you call the matted clumps of fur you find on your dog—other than "matted clumps of fur"? How about that mystery glop they sometimes offer in the school cafeteria lunch—got a special name for that? There are probably a few things you've already made up names for—family names, your own names, or names your friends have come up with. And I'll bet there are lots of things you haven't come up with names for that ought to have special names. Now's your chance.

Pick words that sound like the things you're trying to describe. And to keep from forgetting these words, why not write them down on paper? You can call your collection of words The (Your Name) Dictionary. Why not? You made up the words. You deserve the credit!

O N E
or more

MATERIALS

✎ Paper, pen or pencil

363

Your Roving Reporter . . . On Mars

O N E
or more

MATERIALS

✐ None; or paper,
pen or pencil

Your assignment: You're a reporter (TV or newspaper—your choice), and you've been sent along on the first commercial flight to Mars. Astronauts have discovered a colony of Martian natives living in underground caves on the red planet, and your employer has sent you to interview them and bring back an exclusive.

What questions will you ask them? Try to think of at least fifteen good ones (more is fine, too!). If you wish, write the questions on paper.

If you're doing this with another child, your friend can play the part of a Martian and answer the questions as you ask them.

Zoo's Who?

This activity isn't for everyone; it's for kids with some degree of ability to draw, a sense of humor, and an enjoyment of wordplay. The challenge: to draw pictures of animals whose names are plays on words. (Your child can first think of what the animals are himself, or you can give him the names and just let him come up with the drawings.)

For instance, he might draw a giraft, an elefan, and a posse-um. In my mind, a giraft has a broad, flat back, suitable for carrying a couple of kids downriver; an elefan has a Japanese-style fan at the end of its trunk (very useful in the heat of the jungle); and posse-ums ride on horseback in groups (perhaps wearing silver stars and six-shooters?).

Your child, of course, may envision and depict the animals totally differently.

ONE
or more

MATERIALS

✐ Paper, crayons

Index

Nature activities

Number activities

Card activities

370

One child activities

Two or more children activities

Three or more children activities

Notes

Notes

Notes

Notes